GrossyPelosi is your best friend in the kitchen—actually, he's family.

In his debut cookbook, larger-than-life personality Dan Pelosi offers up a warm hug of home cooking, sharing both comfort and connection with 101 of his nearest and dearest Italian American recipes. Some have been passed down through his family, and others have been cooked up from scratch—but all are made with love and accompanied by fun, meaningful stories to warm your heart while filling your belly. Read how Bimpy (the 100-year-old grandpa the internet loves to love!) smuggled homemade subs into Yankee Stadium, then craft your ultimate **BIG ITALIAN SANDWICH**. Relive the memory of Dan learning how to make his friend's mom's stuffed chicken cutlets in their Jersey Shore house (and getting himself adopted into their family), then level up with **PROSCIUTTO & MOZZARELLA–STUFFED CHICKEN PARM**. Learn how Dan's mom would spring him out of school before the final bell (just to preheat the oven), then make your own **EARLY DISMISSAL POT ROAST**. And rewind to the beginning of Dan's relationship with his boyfriend, Gus, then recreate the **ZABAGLIONE** (and the romantic Cheesecake Factory ambience) that inspired their first "I love you."

In addition to the staple chapters like Eggs, Appetizers, Pasta, Meat & Fish, and Sweets, you'll also find deep dives on Dough and Marinara, presented with hero recipes you can spin into all kinds of deliciousness. (Don't worry—his viral **VODKA SAWCE** is here!) Also sprinkled throughout are Grossy's Guides to cooking, cleaning, organizing, and everything you need to become intuitive in your kitchen.

Approachable and tasty, Dan's recipes are meant to be shared with the ones you love. Set the table, grab a chair, roll up your sleeves . . . now *LET'S EAT*!

LET'S EAT

LET'S EAT

101 Recipes to Fill Your Heart & Home

DAN PELOSI

PHOTOGRAPHS BY ANDREW BUI

U

UNION
SQUARE
& CO.

NEW YORK

UNION SQUARE & CO.
NEW YORK

UNION SQUARE & CO. and the distinctive Union Square & Co. logo are
trademarks of Sterling Publishing Co., Inc.
Union Square & Co., LLC, is a subsidiary of Sterling Publishing Co., Inc.

ISBN 978-1-4549-4639-7 (HC)
ISBN 978-1-4549-5361-6 (BSE)
ISBN 978-1-4549-4640-3 (e-book)

For information about custom editions, special sales, and premium
purchases, please contact specialsales@unionsquareandco.com.

Editor: Amanda Englander
Editorial Assistant: Caroline Hughes
Designer: Laura Palese
Photographer: Andrew Bui
Food Stylist: Tiffany Schleigh
Prop Stylist: Stephanie De Luca
Photography Director: Jennifer Halper
Creative Director: Melissa Farris
Copy Editor: Terry Deal
Proofreaders: Erin Slonaker, Alison Skrabek
Production Editor: Lindsay Herman
Production Manager: Kevin Iwano
Indexer: Elizabeth Parson
Publicist: Erica Gelbard

Printed in China

10 9 8 7 6 5 4 3 2

unionsquareandco.com

For Bimpy

Contents

No One Gets Old at the Table

"A tavola non s'invecchia!" I can still hear my uncle Tony yelling at me across the dinner table during long family dinners. This phrase translates to "no one gets old at the table," meaning that when we eat together, time literally stops—so don't rush. Slow down. Enjoy yourself. When Uncle Tony shouted this, he was usually trying to get me to focus on what was in front of me: our family and the meal we were eating. It was a little lofty for me to understand when I was a kid, but as I've gotten older (turns out we do get old *away* from the table), I live in Uncle Tony's words, sharing food with people I love and finding that magic space where time stands still. I believe food is the great equalizer, and when it's made with care and intention, you can taste the love in every bite.

Let me back up. I'm Dan Pelosi, the Italian American meatball behind the Instagram handle @GrossyPelosi, and a few of my favorite things are comfort and cooking. When I was growing up, most of the kids I knew spent their time outside getting into trouble or in their bedrooms exploring imaginary worlds. Not me. I spent my time in the kitchen with anyone in my family who happened to be cooking . . . which was everyone.

My mom had me on the counter next to the KitchenAid as a toddler while she whipped up elaborate

feasts. Soon I moved from the counter to a stool, then from the stool to the floor. I listened, learned, helped, and definitely made a mess along the way. During the week, I did my homework at the kitchen table after school while my dad made dinner. From memory, he cooked the dishes he had been eating since his childhood, telling me stories the whole time. We tasted everything together, comparing notes and ideas.

Like many Italian American families, my grandparents had a working kitchen in their basement, in addition to the one on the main floor of the house. I spent hours sitting on the stairs with my sister, Diana, watching as my dad's parents, Bimpy and Grandma Katherine, cooked enough food to feed an army. Lucky me, I got to be their official taste tester. In another basement kitchen, literally next door, my mom's parents, Grandma Millie and Grandpa John, let me make "yuck cakes," which involved running around, grabbing anything I could find, stirring it together, and baking it. Grandpa John bravely tasted all my concoctions, no matter what. One set of grandparents gave me the knowledge and palate for Italian American cooking, while the other set gave me the courage to experiment and make mistakes.

During college, I studied abroad in Rome, shopping at the famous Campo de' Fiori market and making family meals for my fellow students. In my twenties and thirties, I spent full weekends cooking for friends, playing the role of Vacation House Mom on group trips, planning holiday events and dinner parties, and creating a comfortable space where my own version of family could gather around the table. Many of my friends call me "Mom" or "Dad" (I answer to both), which, to me, affirms that all the traditions my family passed along are alive and well in me.

When New York City went into lockdown in March 2020, as COVID-19 swept across the world, I immediately turned to my well-stocked pantry and passed the time how I always had: by cooking! I used my Instagram account to share my day-to-day and meal-to-meal with my small community—this sharing helped me cope at a difficult time and, as a bonus, provided comfort to others feeling

anxious and unsure. As the weeks wore on and my audience began to grow, it became clear that, having spent much of my life in the kitchen learning how to comfort and cook, I was uniquely positioned to help people get through a global pandemic. Soon my Instagram account expanded into a website, merch line, collaborations, and brand sponsorships. It's an unusually timed trajectory that I still haven't fully processed, but every day I'm grateful that I get to do what I've always loved to do.

People always ask how I got the name GrossyPelosi. The Drew Barrymore movie *Never Been Kissed* came out when I was in college; after we saw it, all my friends began adoringly calling me "GrossyPelosi" as an homage to the film's main character, Josie Grossy. Needless to say, it stuck! I think it's hysterical and speaks to my brand of living, laughing, and loving.

Seeing as I am a creature of the internet, I naturally love the instant connection of social media. I have a hot-and-heavy relationship with my phone, always responding to comments and DMs on the fly. But a book is a physical thing with no option to DM, so I can't be as available to you as I would like. Think of my recipes as your guides, helping you get where you want to go, but with plenty of room for

you to explore, get lost, discover something new, and then find your way home, happily. Sprinkled throughout the book, you'll also find Grossy's Guides, which are meant to teach you the basics, answer the questions I anticipate you might have, and help you become the very best home cook you can be. I hope you feel as if I'm right there with you, talking you through every step of the way. And if you find yourself stuck, just @ me!

After a lifetime of talking about food with my grandparents, parents, aunts, uncles, and sister, you would think we had nothing more to say. But while writing this book, I spent even more time discussing recipes with every one of those people, soaking up all of our family knowledge, stories, and secrets. This book is dedicated to keeping alive the traditions, the laughter, the conversations, and the recipes of all the generations before me. It's a collection of my favorite recipes—some old, some new, but all rooted in the joy of cooking. They have served me well as simple, approachable, and delicious, ready to be shared with the people I love. And now they're yours to do the same—to adapt, adjust, and scribble notes all over until they feel like your own, and, even if just for a moment, your table will become a place where time stands still.

On the Table

We've talked a lot about me the last few pages, so let's talk about you and your needs as you get ready to cook.

But back to me for one more second: The Grossy way of cooking is to make a mess, encourage mistakes, find creative solutions, eat everything you make (it's how you learn!), scribble notes in the margins, fold down page corners, and always share your love of cooking with those around you. I want you to feel successful and supported on every page of this book, so let's talk about some key info before you dive in.

GROSSY GUIDES

Sprinkled throughout the book are helpful guides that provide the tools you need for success in your day-to-day cooking. Remembering everything all the time is hard, so I love having information where I can easily find it. Whether you are a beginner or a well-seasoned home cook, I hope you'll find these guides filled with useful info and helpful reminders.

RECIPE

Read through the entire recipe before getting started . . . then read it again. Cooking is much less stressful when you know where you're going and how to get there. You'll also find it helpful to know if something needs to braise for four hours, chill in the fridge overnight, or tastes better the longer it sits. Subs and swaps are encouraged because you know best what makes you happy. And please, use the room in the margins to jot down notes for next time! I left it there for you.

THE HEROES

You will find three of my favorite hero recipes in this book: It Doesn't Get Batter Than This (page 67), The Only Dough You'll Knead (page 123), and Grossy's Marinara (page 153). (There's also a surprise on page 147—it's my idea of a sexy centerfold.) What makes them heroic? These recipes are as easy as they are iconic and they're meant to be used over and over again, in multiple ways, while you look like the absolute queen that you are.

GET READY

On the next page, you'll find a list of everything I like to keep on deck. But even a stocked pantry can have missing pieces, so it's important to round everything up before you turn on the stove. You'll also want to take care of any ingredient prep so you're flowing with the recipe, not playing catch-up! And remember, store-bought is always fine. Any recipes here that include a homemade component also have a store-bought option. Both are the right answer, and the outcome will be equally delicious either way.

MOST IMPORTANT

Have fun and spread joy! (And tag me on Instagram.)

Now... Let's Eat!

The Grossery List

The Grossery List is my collection of no-fail items I keep in my kitchen at all times. When the pantry items run out, I replace them on the next grocery run—simply put, I am never without these things. It's an easy system that keeps my kitchen sane and allows me to cook on the fly. Also included here is what I consider must-have equipment. You don't need me to tell you exactly what brand you must have of every single thing—it's just not that involved. Get your hands on what you can, figure out what you like, and the rest will work itself out. Don't get your pantry in a bunch. That's my motto and I'm sticking to it!

Ingredients

BAKING

Active dry yeast
Cocoa powder
Cornstarch
Extracts
- Almond
- Vanilla

Flours
- All-purpose
- Bread

Nutella
Sugars
- Granulated
- Light brown
- Powdered

WINE & LIQUOR

Marsala wine
Red wine
White wine
Vodka

ODDS & ENDS

Anchovies
Honey
Lemons
Mayonnaise
Nuts
- Almonds
- Walnuts
- Pistachios

Pepperoncini
Raisins
Spicy brown mustard

DRY GOODS

Broths
- Chicken
- Vegetable

Canned beans
- Cannellini
- Chickpeas
- Sweet peas

Canned tomatoes, crushed and pureed
Castelvetrano olives, jarred
Polenta
Panko breadcrumbs
Pasta, dried
- Ditalini
- Linguine
- Orecchiette
- Paccheri
- Pastina
- Rigatoni
- Spaghetti

Tomato paste

OILS

Everyday olive oil, for cooking
Special olive oil, for drizzling
Vegetable oil

VINEGARS

Balsamic
Red wine

FRIDGE

Cheeses
- Cream cheese
- Mascarpone
- Parmesan or pecorino
- Whole-milk ricotta

Eggs *(Note: This book uses large eggs for all recipes.)*
Fresh herbs
- Mint
- Chives
- Parsley

Heavy cream
Full-fat sour cream
Unsalted butter
Whole milk

SPICES AND SEASONINGS

Calabrian chili paste
Capers
Dried oregano
Fennel seeds
Garlic cloves
Red pepper flakes
Salt
- Flaky sea salt
- Kosher salt *(Note: This book uses Diamond Crystal kosher salt for all recipes.)*

Whole black peppercorns

Equipment

9 x 5-inch loaf pans
9 x 13-inch baking dish
Bar Keepers Friend
Blender
Cast-iron skillet
5½ quart Dutch oven
Food processor
Knives
- Bread
- Chef's
- Paring

Mandoline (I call mine Amanda Lynne)
Microplane grater
Sheet pans
Spider strainer
Stand mixer or electric hand mixer
Thermometers
- Instant-read
- Frying
- Oven

Wooden spoons (My favorite has a smile on its face)

One of the most common questions I get about my recipes is "How many people does this serve?" My response is usually something like, "The only way I can answer that is if you provide me with bios of everyone at your party as well as the entire menu." This response is not ideal, I know. I have a hard time with serving sizes, because if a pound of pasta tastes really good (like it does with my Vodka Sawce on page 193), then I can easily eat it all by myself! So I always treat serving sizes as a suggestion. But when I am cooking for a crowd, here's what I always consider:

Who's on your GUEST LIST?

I am going to guess that if you are hosting people in your home, you know most of them fairly well. I try to take note of what kinds of eaters my friends and family are, not to judge them, but so I can better serve them. I like my big eaters (anyone with the last name Pelosi) to be well-fed and my more casual eaters not to be overwhelmed.

What's on the MENU?

Are your guests going to fill up on a cheese plate while you cook, or will they be greeted and seated immediately for dinner? What part of the meal is your favorite and what do you want them to focus on? If you spent hours on a gorgeous dessert, maybe it's okay to risk running short on your main course so everyone has room for the sweet stuff! Not all parts of the meal need to be equal, so think strategically about how you want to parse it out. Don't worry—I got you. I've included mix-and-match menus for every occasion on page 19 to make your life easier.

EVERYONE LOVES LEFTOVERS!

My greatest fear in life is not having enough food when I'm hosting. And my greatest joy in life is leftovers. Thank goddess for that, because it is genetically impossible for me *not* to create leftovers when I am cooking. It's a family tradition. So go ahead and double that recipe! I always stock up on reusable containers for my guests to take food home with them.

What do I do with my leftovers? Well, I am glad you asked . . . ➡

GROSSY'S GUIDE TO STORING LEFTOVERS

As an Italian American, a few things always hold true for me: no food goes to waste; there is always someone to feed; and you must make a pregnant person lasagna to keep in the freezer for after the baby comes. Of course, you can find many lovely things to do with leftover food, but if you're looking for a way to use yours, here's everything I know about where to put them:

COUNTER

I generally like to keep my counter nice and clean—a cutting board and my condiment carousel are my only regulars. But a few welcome friends make appearances here and there, stopping by to say hello. Extra baked goods, nicely wrapped up with cling wrap or in airtight containers, find a welcome (if short-lived) respite on the counter. But when life hands you stale bread, make breadcrumbs (page 33)—trust me.

FRIDGE

The fridge is where most leftovers head first; even some things that don't need to be refrigerated end up in the fridge, and that is okay. Better safe than sorry, I say! I am frequently asked if a recipe leftover is worth saving and how long it will last in the fridge. There is no way I can answer that question in any brevity here, but, of course, I have a few general guidelines:

LEFTOVERS ARE LEFTOVERS: They are never going to taste the same as last night's dinner, and thus should not be treated with the same expectations. Leftovers may not reach their full potential if you don't consider a new way to use them. Do they need to be reheated or can they be enjoyed cold? Do they need some new friends to join the party? Maybe 2 slices of bread and a few condiments (page 146 for more on that)! Should they go into a salad? Should pasta be reheated in a pot on the stove, or should you fry it in some oil so it gets crispy? Think outside the Tupperware.

CONSIDER THE INGREDIENTS: The best way to decide how long your leftovers will last in the fridge is to go through the ingredients used to make it. The ingredient that spoils fastest (like fresh herbs or cheese) should dictate the eat-by date for the entire dish. A great example is homemade pesto: oil and nuts can last a loooong time, but the chopped basil will brown and die pretty quickly, so you'll want to finish your pesto before that happens.

FOLLOW YOUR NOSE! Not a day goes by that I don't grab something from my fridge, remove its lid, and smell it! If it smells okay, it will be okay to eat. If it doesn't, toss it!

FREEZER

Only a few people know that Bimpy's full name is Bimpy Freezer King. This is thanks to the sheer number of freezers—at one point there were five—in his basement, including one gigantic lay-down freezer, which we lovingly joked could house a few dead bodies. My dad recently found a pound of butter from 1967 in one freezer, which tells you how serious Bimpy is about freezing food for later. (Don't worry, we threw it out.) Here is everything I learned about what to freeze and how to freeze it:

SOME FREEZING ADVICE. While some food can last in the freezer for even longer, a maximum of three months is a great rule to follow. I always label freezer leftovers so I know what it is and on what date it became a leftover.

SLICE AND DICE. Consider cutting everything up before you freeze it. That way you can defrost only what you need at any given moment—plus, smaller portions defrost faster anyway. Cut extra bread into toastable pieces. Individual servings of frozen Eggplant Parmesan (page 166) make a mean last-minute dinner.

THAT'S A WRAP. My mother is an evangelist for wrapping food thoroughly and tightly before freezing it. At some point in my childhood, she bought one of these vacuum sealers for food because she simply does not mess around. I will never forget the look on the leftovers' faces as they were suffocated at the hand of my own mother. That said, you do not need a food vacuum—you just need to take a moment to wrap everything nice and tight using cling wrap and freezer bags so that your food comes back to life fresh and ready for you to reheat and enjoy.

I am all about cooking on the fly, making the most with what I have around, and not stressing out when I forget something at the store or can't find my measuring spoons. You can find a way to make most things work, I promise, and this guide will help you figure out how.

Volume Conversions						
TEASPOONS	TABLESPOONS	OUNCES	CUPS	PINTS	QUARTS	GALLONS
3	1	½				
6	2	1	⅛			
12	4	2	¼			
24	8	4	½	¼		
48	16	8	1	½	¼	
		16	2	1	½	
		32	4	2	1	¼
		64	8	4	2	½
		128	16	8	4	1

Weight Conversions		
OUNCES	GRAMS	POUNDS
2	58	
4	114	
6	170	
8	226	½
12	340	
16	454	1

DASH = 1/16 teaspoon

PINCH = 1/18 teaspoon

Common Substitutions

ITEM	AMOUNT	SUBSTITUTE
Baking powder	1 teaspoon	¼ teaspoon baking soda + ½ teaspoon lemon juice
Baking soda	1 teaspoon	3 teaspoons baking powder
Breadcrumbs	1 cup	1 cup cracker crumbs
Brown sugar	1 cup	1 cup granulated sugar + 1 tablespoon molasses
Butter *(for baking)*	1 stick	1 mashed banana
Buttermilk	1 cup	1 cup whole milk + 1 tablespoon lemon juice
Cake flour	1 cup	Sift 14 tablespoons all-purpose flour + 2 tablespoons cornstarch
Cornstarch	1 tablespoon	1 tablespoon instant mashed potatoes or 2 tablespoons all-purpose flour
Cream of tartar	¼ teaspoon	¼ teaspoon lemon juice + ¼ teaspoon distilled white vinegar
Egg	1 large	½ mashed banana or ¼ cup applesauce
Fresh herbs	1 tablespoon	1 teaspoon dried herbs
Heavy cream	1 cup	1 cup milk + 1 tablespoon melted butter
Mayonnaise	1 cup	1 cup Greek yogurt
Whole milk	1 cup	1 cup half-and-half or 1 cup sour cream or 1 cup canned coconut milk or ½ cup heavy cream + ½ cup water
Oil *(for baking)*	1 cup	1 cup applesauce
Red wine	1 cup	1 cup beef broth or vegetable bouillon
Sour cream	1 cup	1 cup Greek yogurt
Tomato puree	1 cup	½ cup tomato paste + ½ cup water or 1 cup blended whole or diced tomatoes from a can
Vinegar, any kind	½ teaspoon	1 teaspoon lemon juice
White wine	1 cup	1 cup chicken broth or vegetable bouillon

I'm all about making recipes work for you and swapping things out to taste and preference to include the food you love. And while I am many things, I am not a dietitian! Any serious food allergies or intolerances should be discussed with a professional. You probably already know the best subs and your favorite brands, but let's quickly discuss some easy substitutions in this book.

The recipes in this book use whole milk, but any plant-based milk—almond, oat, soy, coconut, and so on—will work in its place. You can also swap in dairy-free butter for all recipes, savory and sweet. Plant-based cheeses have come a long way, and most are an easy swap for any dairy cheese.

Gluten-free pasta will work for all the recipes in this book. Same for gluten-free flour in place of all-purpose. Gluten-free 1:1 baking flour is perfect for any recipes that use baking powder and/or baking soda and can be used in the exact same amount. Gluten-free all-purpose flour works better with any yeasted recipes, also in an equal amount.

An abundance of recipes here are naturally vegetarian, but for anything that uses meat, feel free to get creative with plant-based substitutes or hearty vegetables, like mushrooms, squash, or eggplant. Vegetable broth can always be substituted for meat-based broth.

GROSSY'S GUIDE TO MENU PLANNING

I am often asked for the ideal recipe for any, every, and very specific occasions—nothing makes me happier than playing matchmaker between an excited cook and the perfect dish! Below are some typical entertaining situations with lots of options to mix and match. I promise, each of them will send your guests home feeling full and happy.

EVERYONE IS VEGETARIAN

Spinach & Mushroom Baked Eggs	60
Bimpy's Escarole & Beans	99
Four Seasons Salad	103
Mom's Stuffed Artichokes	112
Whole-Roasted Eggplant with Calabrian Chili Crisp	119
Mushroom Bolognese	190

ALL I HAVE IS MY PANTRY

Spaghetti Aglio e Olio	177
Ceci e Pepe	181
Bimpy's Pasta e Piselli	185
Olive Oil Ice Cream	267
Grandma Katherine's Rice Pudding	276

IT'S WEDNESDAY— WTF IS FOR DINNER?

Eggs in Purgatory	42
Broccoli Rabe & Sausage Pasta	186
Fork & Knife Carbonara	189
Bean, Kale & Linguiça Skillet	215
Sausage & Peppers & Potatoes & Onions	226
Chicken Marsala	234

I'M TOO LAZY TO COOK

Pastina: The Italian Cure-All	49
Leftover Pasta Frittata	59
Marinated Tomato Toast	86
Fresh Corn Polenta	107
Tiramisu Affogato	279

I WANT TO SPEND ALL DAY IN THE KITCHEN

Mom's Italian Bread	92
Sunday Ragù	170
Early Dismissal Pot Roast	219
Porchetta	221
Cuccidati for Grandma Millie	261
Rainbow Cookie Loaf Cake	271

I HAVE TO FEED A CROWD

Italian Baked Potato Bar	108
Bimpy's Pizza	132
The Big Italian Sandwich	145
Prosciutto & Mozzarella–Stuffed Chicken Parm	168
Italian Holiday Cookies	255
Torta del Diavolo	280

I WANT TO MAKE IT ALL AHEAD

Sheet Pan Breakfast Sandwich	45
Pepper & Egg Strata	52
Quattro Formaggi Quiche	53
Four-Cheese Lasagna	165
Chocolate Anise Biscotti	249
Zabaglione	283

I WANT A PROPOSAL

Italian Gay Wedding Soup	85
Grossy's Vodka Sawce	193
Spicy Linguine with Clams	209
Piri Piri Roast Chicken	225
Tagliata di Manzo	237
Aunt Chris's Cheesecake	247

I WANT MY IN-LAWS TO LOVE ME

Roasted Fennel, Orange & Olive Salad	115
Gigantic Meatballs	162
Eggplant Parmesan	166
Shrimp Scampi over Polenta	233
Whole Branzino with Tricolore Slaw	241
Pistachio Bundt Cake	275

I WAS ASKED TO A POTLUCK DINNER

Decline the invitation.

When it comes to cleaning her house, my mom is an unmatched force—except maybe by my sister, who is equally intense. The two of them will clean you out of house and home. In fact, when they come to visit me, they do. Some of you are probably thinking, *Dan's mom should meet my mom, no one cleans like her.* And you are absolutely right, no one cleans quite like your own mom. Others of you are probably thinking, *My mom did not clean a thing, please help!* This guide is for children of dust busters and dust bunnies alike. I asked my mom to list her best cleaning tips, thinking she would type them up and email them. Instead, a few days later, she handed me an envelope with handwritten instructions on folded notepad paper. That dossier is transcribed for you here, word for word.

Cleaning Your OVEN

Combine 1 cup distilled white vinegar and 2 cups water in an ovenproof pot. Set the oven temperature to 350°F and leave the pot in the oven for 20 minutes or up to an hour. Remove the pot and turn off the oven. Once the oven is cool, wipe it clean.

Cleaning Your FRIDGE

Fill a spray bottle with ¼ cup distilled white vinegar and 2 cups water. Spray and wipe the fridge, inside and outside. Old socks work well for wiping.

Cleaning Your SINK

Plug the sink. Add 2 tablespoons baking soda and plenty of water and let it soak. Drain and it sparkles. For tougher stains, like rust, lime stains, and tarnish, apply Bar Keepers Friend with a soft cloth or sponge. Rinse well.

Cleaning Your FAUCET

To clean buildup on the faucet, fill a plastic sandwich bag with apple cider vinegar and a few drops of essential oil (optional, but it smells nice). Secure the bag over the faucet with a rubber band and leave it overnight. Rinse in the morning and all grime will be gone!

Cleaning Your COUNTERTOPS

Fill a spray bottle with ¼ cup distilled white vinegar and 2 cups water. Spray and wipe with a soft cloth daily.

Cleaning Your DISHWASHER

When the dishwasher begins to smell, I add 2 tablespoons baking soda and 2 cups distilled white vinegar to the bottom of the basin. Let that sit for 20 minutes, then run a rinse cycle.

Cleaning Your MICROWAVE

Combine ½ cup distilled white vinegar and 1 cup water in a microwave-safe bowl. Place the bowl in the microwave and turn the microwave on high for 1 minute. Remove the bowl and wipe down the insides of the microwave with a soft cloth. The old sock works well here, too.

Cleaning Your DUTCH OVENS, PANS, & SHEET PANS

Always let pans cool before cleaning or the bottom will warp and the pans will no longer lie flat on the burner. For light cleaning, use Dawn dish soap. Heavier cleaning calls for Bar Keepers Friend. The heaviest cleaning requires soaking overnight with water and kosher salt and rinsing in the morning. Stuck-on food sometimes calls for boiling a mixture of water and white vinegar in the pan on the stovetop, which works well to loosen up the food and stains before washing.

Cleaning Your KITCHEN CABINETS

Add 1 capful Murphy's Oil Soap to 1 gallon warm water. Wipe the cabinets with a soft cloth. This also works well on woodwork, baseboards, and wooden doors.

Cleaning Your HARDWOOD FLOORS

Combine ½ cup Windex and 1 gallon water. Wash the floors with the mixture—a Swiffer fitted with another old sock works great.

DUSTING Your Everything

Wear old wool gloves to use as dust cloths so you can easily get everywhere, especially around hard shapes or all those knickknacks. Throw them in the laundry and use them again and again. Once a month, spray Pledge on the gloves.

Removing STAINS FROM YOUR CLOTHES

In a spray bottle, combine one part blue Dawn dish soap and two parts 3% hydrogen peroxide. Spray directly on the stain. Use a dedicated laundry toothbrush to gently rub the solution into your stains. Launder as usual and watch the stains disappear. If all else fails, put Lestoil on the spots and soak it for a couple hours in clean water. Wash as usual. Even if stains have been there for years, this works!

NOTE from Grossy

I always say that stains on your clothes are the sign of a life well-lived, and I wear them with pride and joy. After years of watching me wipe my sauce-covered hands on everything and dropping food all over myself, my mom came up with the absolute best way to hit reset on an outfit. While the stains may disappear, the pride lasts forever.

Dressings, Toppings & Spreads

Herbs are nature's condiments. They're a small touch, but when matched just right, herbs help soups, stews, dips, meats, sauces, and veggies come alive. Below is my guide to the ones I reach for most often and my favorite ways to use them. Remember, dried herbs are super concentrated in flavor, so use about one-third of the amount of fresh when substituting.

HERB	KEEPING IT FRESH	STAR POWER
Basil	Rinse and dry, then trim the stems and store upright on the counter with the stems in a few inches of water for about a week. Don't forget to change the water every couple of days!	The prima donna of Italian cooking, basil is the perfect partner for all things tomato. Also a great supporting player for meat and vegetables.
Bay Leaves	Wrap in damp paper towels and store refrigerated in a zip-top bag for up to 10 days.	Fresh bay leaves have an almost menthol flavor and are the rare instance where fresh is stronger than dried. Soups, stocks, and anything brothy loves a bay leaf. (Just remember to fish her out before serving!)
Chives	Rinse, dry, and wrap in damp paper towels. Store in a zip-top bag in the fridge for up to 10 days.	Eggs, fish, potatoes, and dips all benefit from the light oniony bite of fresh chives. Because the flavor is so delicate, it's best to use these as a garnish.
Fennel	Rinse and dry, then trim the stalks and store upright on the counter in a few inches of water for a week. Don't forget to change the water every couple of days!	Fennel is an incredible plant—from the seeds to the bulb to the green fronds on top. The delicate anise flavor is a perfect touch in fresh salads or roasted and served alongside rich meats.
Mint	Rinse and dry, then trim the stems and place upright with the stems in a few inches of water. Cover loosely with a zip-top bag and store refrigerated for about a week. Don't forget to change the water every couple of days!	Mint has long been a reigning champ in desserts, but it's your secret weapon in savory cooking, too. Fatty meats and charred veggies benefit from its cool freshness.
Oregano	Rinse and dry, then wrap in damp paper towels. Store refrigerated in a zip-top bag for up to a week.	Fresh oregano has a very different flavor from dried and plays well with fish, chicken, and tomatoes.
Parsley	Rinse and dry, then trim the stems and place upright with the stems in a few inches of water. Cover loosely with a zip-top bag and store refrigerated for about a week. Don't forget to change the water every couple of days!	Parsley and pasta? Name a more iconic duo. Anything meaty, fatty, or carby also loves an herbaceous parsley punch.
Rosemary	Rinse and dry, then wrap in damp paper towels. Store refrigerated in a zip-top bag for up to a week.	Woodsy and pungent, rosemary makes everything taste richer. Stews, roasted meat, and hearty veggies all want some rosemary in their lives.
Thyme	Rinse and dry, then wrap in damp paper towels. Store refrigerated in a zip-top bag for up to a week or more.	Thyme's fresh and citrus-like flavor feels like it was engineered for the ultimate eggs, soups, beans, fish, chicken—I could go on, but we don't have the thyme.

Calabrian Chili Crisp

I spend so much of my time re-creating food memories from my childhood—the taste, the smell, the feeling. My strongest and oldest food memory is this: I was seven years old, sitting in the basement kitchen of my uncle Tony's, just down the street from Bimpy's house. (Somehow my entire family lived on the same street.) I ate a bowl of the most amazingly seasoned tomatoey masterpiece; the combo of herbs and spices almost knocked me over. To this day, I cannot remember the dish, but I have spent my life on a quest to re-create its depth of flavor. This Calabrian Chili Crisp takes me back to that basement kitchen. The Italian classics (garlic, rosemary, fennel seeds) are accented by some surprising additions (cumin and celery seeds), but the end result is a thick, oily, perfectly spicy condiment that is a must-have in every kitchen. It sets the standard for everything I cook.

PUT HER TO WORK

Sheet Pan Breakfast Sandwich (page 45)
Pepper & Egg Strata (page 52)
Spinach & Mushroom Baked Eggs (page 60)
Italian Baked Potato Bar (page 108)
Whole-Roasted Eggplant with Calabrian Chili Crisp (page 119)
Focaccia (page 137)

Note

Add more (or use less) Calabrian chili paste to give this crisp the perfect level of heat that makes you happy.

Makes 1½ cups

6 garlic cloves, thinly sliced	1 tablespoon fresh thyme leaves
1 medium shallot, thinly sliced	1 tablespoon tomato paste
1 cup extra-virgin olive oil	1 tablespoon Calabrian chili paste
1 tablespoon sugar	¾ teaspoon kosher salt
1 tablespoon fennel seeds	½ teaspoon cumin seeds
1 tablespoon minced fresh rosemary leaves	½ teaspoon celery seeds

1. In a small saucepan, combine the garlic, shallot, and olive oil. Set the saucepan over low heat and let the garlic and shallot sizzle away, stirring occasionally, until deeply browned and crisp, 10 to 12 minutes.

2. While these girls sizzle, in a medium bowl, combine the sugar, fennel seeds, rosemary, thyme, tomato paste, chili paste, salt, cumin seeds, and celery seeds. Pour the contents of the pan, including the oil, into the bowl. Whisk to combine well.

3. Let the mixture cool completely, about 30 minutes, then transfer it to an airtight container and store refrigerated for up to 2 weeks. Let the chili crisp sit at room temperature to loosen up before using.

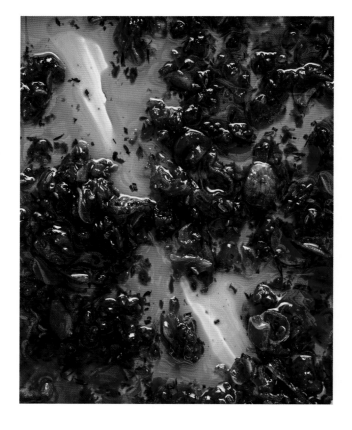

Balsamic Drizzle

Balsamic vinegar was the absolute superstar of the '90s. She came out of nowhere (well, she came out of Italy) and suddenly all my mom's friends were talking about her like she wasn't there on the table, just waiting to be held. Like many other things from that decade, she's back again! Because this recipe is made with literally one ingredient, make it count with the best balsamic you can manage. As the vinegar boils down, it begins to lean sweeter, thicker, bigger, and bolder, making it a perfect finishing drizzle on veggies, salads, meats, and even ice cream if you swing that way.

Makes 1 cup

1 (16.9-ounce) bottle balsamic vinegar

1. Heat the vinegar in a small saucepan over high heat. As soon as the vinegar comes to a boil, reduce the heat to medium and simmer until very syrupy and reduced to about ½ cup, 30 to 35 minutes.

2. Pour the glaze into an airtight container and let it cool with the lid off for 30 minutes. Cover tightly and store at room temperature for up to 1 month.

PUT HER TO WORK
Sheet Pan Breakfast Sandwich (page 45)
Marinated Tomato Toast (page 86)
Focaccia (page 137)
Tagliata di Manzo (page 237)

Citrusy Olive Tapenade

When I lived in San Francisco in my twenties, my favorite restaurant started putting plates of warm olives with orange rinds on their menus as a starter, and I immediately fell in love with the combo of citrus, fat, and salt. My version of tapenade is a memory of that first magic moment. The usual suspects, like parsley, basil, capers, and olives, get a surprise accent with orange zest that just feels so right. I want to eat it olive of the time. And for the anchovy-afraid out there, trust me that they blend right in and make this the salty, briny, savory spread of your dreams. Also, Olive Tapenade is a great drag name in a pinch.

Makes 3 cups

2 cups loosely packed fresh parsley leaves	2 cups pitted kalamata olives
1 cup loosely packed fresh basil leaves	1 cup pitted Castelvetrano olives
4 anchovy fillets	¼ cup drained capers
	Zest of 1 orange (optional)

1. In a food processor, combine the parsley, basil, and anchovies. Pulse about 5 times, until the herbs are nicely minced. Add all the olives and the capers and pulse 6 to 8 more times, stopping to scrape down the sides as needed, until the olives are finely chopped.

2. Transfer the mixture to a small bowl and stir in the orange zest (if using).

3. Refrigerate in an airtight container for up to 1 week.

PUT HER TO WORK
Italian Baked Potato Bar (page 108)
Focaccia (page 137)

Basil Almond Pesto

It was the pesto times, it was . . . well, the pesto times. We like to keep things positive here, folks! Pesto is an absolute breeze to make, and there are endless ways to make it your own. Trust me, I have made them all! The key is nailing your ratios: a perfect balance of greens, nuts, cheese, garlic, and, of course, oil. Use this recipe as the blueprint and go wild tagging in new players. Think pine nuts, walnuts, pistachios, sunflower seeds, or leafy herbs, kale, spinach, celery leaves. The pestobilities are endless! For my money, I think Basil Almond Pesto is my favorite. The roasted almonds add a savory, nutty flavor that makes the classic pesto flavors even more perfect.

Makes 1 ¼ cups

3 cups packed fresh basil leaves

½ cup roasted, unsalted almonds

½ cup freshly grated Parmesan or pecorino cheese

4 garlic cloves

½ teaspoon kosher salt, plus more as needed

½ teaspoon freshly ground black pepper

¼ teaspoon red pepper flakes

½ cup extra-virgin olive oil

1. In a food processor or blender, combine the basil, almonds, Parmesan, garlic, salt, black pepper, and pepper flakes. Pulse 8 to 10 times to break down the ingredients, stopping to scrape down the sides as needed. Slowly drizzle the olive oil into the food processor as you pulse about 4 more times, incorporating it bit by bit into the pesto. Your pesto should look well incorporated and stunningly green. Be sure to check on those almonds—they like to hide and act difficult! I am team chunky pesto, but you can make yours as smooth as you like.

2. Taste the pesto for seasoning, then transfer to an airtight container and store refrigerated for up to a week.

PUT HER TO WORK
Sheet Pan Breakfast Sandwich (page 45)
Italian Baked Potato Bar (page 108)
Bimpy's Pizza (page 132)
Focaccia (page 137)
Pesto Corn Tomato Pasta Salad (page 201)

Note
When using pesto in pasta dishes, reserve some pasta cooking water before you drain it, then return the pasta to the pan and add the pesto directly to it. Slowly add some of that reserved pasta cooking water, about ½ cup at a time, as you stir until your desired creaminess and dreaminess is achieved! Pesto is also delicious in pasta salad, chicken salad, deviled eggs, on all types of meat, on beans, or even as a red sauce sub on pizza.

Fresh Mint Gremolata

I always have extra herbs hanging around my kitchen—therefore I'm always looking for ways to use them up before they die. Gremolata is one of my favorite hacks for doing just that. I love it because it's salty, herby, fresh, and extremely simple. Traditional gremolata is heavy on parsley, but any other tender leaves like basil, chives, cilantro, dill, or tarragon could slip right in here, too. I'm a huge fan of mint, so I make this remixed version most often. Add her to a salad, a sandwich, or an egg, and you'll see it was mint to be!

Makes ½ cup

2 cups loosely packed fresh mint leaves	2 garlic cloves
	Kosher salt
1 cup loosely packed fresh parsley leaves	Zest of 1 lemon
	Juice of ½ lemon

1. In a food processor, combine the mint, parsley, garlic, and a pinch of salt. Process until the garlic and herbs are finely chopped, about 30 seconds. Transfer the mixture to a small bowl.

2. Add the lemon zest and lemon juice and stir to combine. Use the gremolata immediately or cover tightly and refrigerate for up to 2 hours.

PUT HER TO WORK
Sheet Pan Breakfast Sandwich (page 45)
Marinated Zucchini with Gremolata Vinaigrette (page 111)

Herb-Infused Oil

My love affair with herb-infused oil started in the checkout line at Williams Sonoma. (I assume this is where it started for most people, no?) My entire family would get stuck on a tasting loop—rows of oily bowls and perfectly cubed pieces of bread as far as the eye could see. Beyond feeding a family of four during a trip to the mall, herb oil is great for so many other things: put extra herbs to use; make simple pastas a little special; give a classy gift to someone you love . . . you can even use it as a substitute for olive oil! It's worth using high-quality olive oil here—you'll really taste the difference.

Makes about 1 liter

1 (1-liter) bottle extra-virgin olive oil	⅓ cup garlic cloves, smashed
1 bunch thyme sprigs	1 tablespoon whole black peppercorns
4 rosemary sprigs	1 tablespoon dried oregano
2 basil sprigs	

1. In a medium saucepan, combine the olive oil, thyme, rosemary, basil, garlic, peppercorns, and oregano. Set the saucepan over low heat until the oil begins to bubble and you hear a nice little sizzle, about 5 minutes. Cook, stirring occasionally, until the herbs begin to wilt, about 5 minutes more. Remove from the heat and let the oil cool completely in the pan, about 1 hour.

2. Strain the oil through a fine-mesh sieve into a spouted measuring cup or pitcher, discarding the solids. Pour the infused oil back into the 1-liter bottle and close the lid tightly. Store in a cool, dark place for up to 1 month.

PUT HER TO WORK
Homemade Breadcrumbs (page 33)
Eggs in Purgatory (page 42)

Note
A pinch of red pepper flakes adds the perfect spice.

Giardiniera

Bimpy loves to talk about the 25-gallon barrel filled with vegetables that was in his family's basement throughout his childhood. Cauliflower, onions, hot and sweet peppers, all drowning in vinegar, topped with a board and a stone to weigh it all down. The family would dip into the barrel all winter long, and, as Bimpy says, "It was a great way to eat your vegetables!" This recipe for giardiniera does not make enough to fill a 25-gallon barrel (though feel free to scale it up if that's your thing), but it will give you the perfectly punchy vegetables of your dreams and a tangy brine to go with them. Now you have an instant snack, appetizer, or zingy topping for whatever recipe is waiting in your kitchen . . . or your basement?

Makes 1 quart

2 cups cauliflower florets	½ cup kosher salt
2 medium carrots, cut diagonally into ½-inch-thick slices	2 garlic cloves
	1 teaspoon dried oregano
1 celery stalk, cut diagonally into ½-inch-thick slices	1 teaspoon celery seeds
	1 teaspoon whole black peppercorns
2 sweet peppers, cut into ¼-inch-thick rounds	1½ cups distilled white vinegar
2 serrano peppers, thinly sliced (optional)	½ cup extra-virgin olive oil, plus more as needed

1. In a quart-sized glass jar, combine the cauliflower, carrots, celery, sweet peppers, serrano peppers (if using), and salt. Fill the jar to the brim with cold water. Close the lid tightly and shake to dissolve the salt. Refrigerate overnight.

2. Drain and rinse the vegetables. Run the jar and lid through the dishwasher or boil in a large pot of water for 10 minutes to sterilize (see note). Let the jar cool. Place the vegetables back into the jar. Grate the garlic directly into the jar, then add the oregano, celery seeds, peppercorns, vinegar, and olive oil. Close the lid tightly and shake to combine well. If needed, add more olive oil to cover the vegetables completely.

3. Store refrigerated for at least 24 hours and up to 2 weeks.

PUT HER TO WORK
Uncle Phil's Deviled Eggs (page 63)
The Big Italian Sandwich (page 145)

Note
This preservation is super low acid, so sterilizing your jar is a must!

Homemade Breadcrumbs

A long-running joke among my friends is that I am actually the witch from the fairy tale "Hansel and Gretel," luring them to my gingerbread house made of cookies and candy so I can fatten them up and eat them. They aren't wrong, except that they know they don't need to leave a trail of breadcrumbs behind them since I always have plenty on hand (oh, also they know that I will not, in fact, try to eat them). Like many of my recipes, this one calls back to the idea of nothing going to waste. A slightly stale, crusty loaf gets a second lease on life as a garlicky, herby, satisfyingly crunchy topping. I can't think of a dish that isn't made better with a little sprinkle of breadcrumbs!

Makes about 2 cups

¼ loaf stale Italian bread	Kosher salt
1 garlic clove, grated	
¼ cup Herb-Infused Oil (page 31) or extra-virgin olive oil	1 teaspoon dried herbs, such as parsley, oregano, and/or basil

1. Preheat the oven to 300°F.

2. Tear the bread into small pieces and arrange on a rimmed sheet pan. Transfer to the oven and bake for 15 to 20 minutes, or until the bread is completely dried out and hardened.

3. Transfer the bread to a food processor and add the garlic. Pulse 6 to 8 times, until the bread is broken down into uneven crumbs. (Some larger pieces are totally welcome at this party.)

4. Heat the oil in a large skillet over medium-low heat. When the oil is shimmering, add the breadcrumbs and a pinch of salt. Toast the crumbs, stirring often, until they're nicely golden brown, about 4 minutes. Remove the skillet from the heat, add the dried herbs, and stir to mix well.

5. Transfer the breadcrumbs to an airtight container. Let cool completely with the lid off, then cover. Store at room temperature for up to 2 weeks.

PUT HER TO WORK
Roasted Fennel, Orange & Olive Salad (page 115)
Gigantic Meatballs (page 162)
Beany Zucchini Balls (page 164)
Sunday Ragù (page 170)
Spaghetti Aglio e Olio (page 177)
Spicy Linguine with Clams (page 209)
Live, Loaf, Love (page 229)

Note
If you have more stale bread, just scale up the other ingredients to make it work. These measurements are forgiving.

Mostarda di Frutta

I am deeply in love with mustard in all forms: yellow, Dijon, deli, brown. . . . But if I had to pick a single condiment on earth that I loved the most as a kid, it has to be honey mustard. So it only makes sense that in adulthood, I've grown into a mostarda di frutta queen. A classic Italian condiment of dried fruits and mustard seed, mostarda di frutta is a beautiful next-level version of that sweet acidity I have loved my whole life. As everything boils together, a thick paste emerges, featuring lots of great texture from the fruit. Sharp, bright, sweet, and a little spicy, she hits all the right notes.

Makes 3 cups

½ cup dried cherries

½ cup dried apricots, roughly chopped

½ cup dried figs, roughly chopped

2 Granny Smith apples, peeled and diced

2 bay leaves

½ cup sugar

½ cup honey

¼ cup spicy brown mustard

2 tablespoons brown or yellow mustard seed

¼ teaspoon red pepper flakes

1. In a large saucepan, combine the cherries, apricots, figs, apples, bay leaves, sugar, honey, mustard, mustard seed, pepper flakes, and 3 cups of water over medium heat. Bring to a simmer and cook, stirring occasionally, until the mixture is reduced by about half, 45 minutes to 1 hour. You should have plump chunks of fruit coated in a thick, gooey syrup.

2. Remove the pan from the heat and let the mixture cool completely, about 1 hour. Transfer to an airtight container and store refrigerated for up to 2 weeks.

PUT HER TO WORK
Baked Brie Bread Bowl (page 78)
Sheet Pan Chicken with Brussels Sprouts (page 230)

Aioli Have Eyes for You

For those new to this party, aioli is a delicious condiment made from a base of garlic and olive oil; it's like mayonnaise, but so much better. Two of my favorites are Bagna Cauda Aioli (henceforth known as BC Aioli), inspired by my love affair with anchovies and all the salty brininess they bring, and Agliata and Porrata Aioli (forevermore AP Aioli), which gets its rich flavor from garlic's sweeter sister, the leek. Both of these girls are meant to be used as toppings, spreads, dipping sauces, or even licked off your finger if you're nasty.

BC Aioli

Makes about 1½ cups

6 garlic cloves

2 (2-ounce) tins anchovies, drained

Juice of ½ lemon

1 egg yolk

1 teaspoon spicy brown mustard

½ teaspoon kosher salt

½ teaspoon freshly ground black pepper

¾ cup vegetable oil

1. In a blender, combine the garlic, anchovies, lemon juice, egg yolk, mustard, salt, and pepper. Blend on low until well incorporated, stopping to scrape down the sides as needed, about 30 seconds.

2. With the blender running on low, gently stream in about half the oil as slowly as possible. Increase the blender speed to medium and continue streaming in the oil until a smooth and thick aioli forms. (Pouring too much oil too fast will make for a runny aioli.)

3. Transfer the aioli to an airtight container and store refrigerated for up to 2 weeks.

PUT HER TO WORK
Sheet Pan Breakfast Sandwich (page 45)
Fritto Misto (page 74)
Italian Baked Potato Bar (page 108)
Mom's Stuffed Artichokes (page 112)

Note

A broken aioli means it's runny and separated, but don't throw it out! Pour the contents into a spouted measuring cup. Rinse out the blender and place another egg yolk in it, then, with the blender running on low, slowly pour the broken aioli back in. When it begins to emulsify, increase the speed to medium and continue pouring until fully incorporated. Voilà!

AP Aioli

Makes about 2 cups

1 tablespoon extra-virgin olive oil

8 garlic cloves, thinly sliced

1 leek, halved and thinly sliced into half-moons

Juice of ½ lemon

1 egg yolk

1 teaspoon spicy brown mustard

¾ teaspoon kosher salt

½ teaspoon freshly ground black pepper

¾ cup vegetable oil

1. In a small skillet, heat the olive oil over low heat. When the oil is shimmering, add the garlic and leek. Cook, stirring occasionally, until the garlic and leek are soft but not yet taking on color, about 10 minutes.

2. Transfer the cooked garlic and leek to a blender. Add the lemon juice, egg yolk, mustard, salt, and pepper. Blend on low until well incorporated, stopping to scrape the sides as needed, about 30 seconds.

3. With the blender running on low, gently stream in about half the oil as slowly as possible. Increase the blender speed to medium and continue streaming in the oil until a smooth and thick aioli forms. (Pouring too much oil too fast will make for a runny aioli.)

4. Transfer the aioli to an airtight container and store refrigerated for up to 2 weeks.

PUT HER TO WORK
Fried Calamari & Pepperoncini (page 69)
Fritto Misto (page 74)
Mom's Stuffed Artichokes (page 112)
Live, Loaf, Love (page 229)

A Tale of Two Confits

When I die, bury me in olive oil and bake me until I am crispy on the outside, creamy on the inside, and tastier than anyone could have ever imagined. Until then, I'll keep making confit. Two things I love having on hand at all times are tomatoes and garlic—but cooked in a low-and-slow oil bath until sweet and ready to burst. This recipe covers the basic how-to, but feel free to remix with herbs and spices like dried oregano, red pepper flakes, fennel seeds, or tons of black pepper. Both versions will quickly become staples in your kitchen—there's little they don't make better.

Tomato Confit

Makes about 4 cups

2 pints cherry tomatoes	1 basil sprig
8 garlic cloves	2½ cups extra-virgin olive oil

1. Preheat the oven to 350°F.

2. In a 9 x 13-inch baking dish, arrange the tomatoes, garlic, and basil snugly in a single layer. Cover the mixture completely with the olive oil.

3. Roast for about 30 minutes, until the tomatoes are soft and just beginning to burst. Or, if you like your tomatoes extra soft, continue roasting for 5 minutes at a time until they hit your dream texture. Remove from the oven and let cool completely, about 1 hour.

4. Discard the basil. Transfer the confit tomatoes, garlic, and oil to an airtight container or jar. Store refrigerated for up to 2 weeks.

PUT HER TO WORK
Sheet Pan Breakfast Sandwich (page 45)
Bimpy's Pizza (page 132)
Focaccia (page 137)

Garlic Confit

Makes about 4 cups

3 cups garlic cloves (see Note)	2½ cups extra-virgin olive oil

1. Preheat the oven to 350°F.

2. In a 9 x 13-inch baking dish arrange the garlic in a single layer. Cover the mixture completely with the olive oil.

3. Roast for about 30 minutes, until the garlic is soft and golden brown. Or, if you like your garlic extra caramelized, continue roasting for 5 minutes at a time until it looks how you like. Remove from the oven and let cool completely, about 1 hour.

4. Transfer the confit garlic and oil to an airtight container or jar. Store refrigerated for up to 2 weeks.

PUT HER TO WORK
Eggs in Purgatory (page 42)
Italian Baked Potato Bar (page 108)
Bimpy's Pizza (page 132)
Focaccia (page 137)

Note
I promise, you do not want to peel this much garlic. Buy it already peeled: about 1 pound will get you 3 cups.

Dress for Success

It's a bold statement, but I would say these dressings may be the only two you need. They're extremely versatile: one minute they're fulfilling your salad dreams and the next they're unlocking your sandwich flavor fantasy. Or maybe on Monday they're marinating your chicken, and by Thursday they're dripping off your roasted veggies. They're everywhere all at once, and they can do all the things. Miss Garlicky Oregano is all herby goodness, earthy and comforting. Miss Garlicky Citrus is spunky with an acidic sense of humor. Whichever girl you befriend, you're gonna be spending a lot of time with her!

Garlicky Oregano Dressing

Makes about ¾ cup

½ cup extra-virgin olive oil

6 garlic cloves

3 tablespoons red wine vinegar

2 tablespoons spicy brown mustard

2 tablespoons dried oregano

½ teaspoon kosher salt, plus more as needed

½ teaspoon freshly ground black pepper, plus more as needed

¼ teaspoon red pepper flakes, plus more as needed

1. In a blender or food processor, combine the olive oil, garlic, vinegar, mustard, oregano, salt, black pepper, and pepper flakes. Blend on high until well combined, about 30 seconds. Taste for seasoning.

2. Transfer to an airtight container and store refrigerated for up to 1 week.

PUT HER TO WORK
Pelosi Family Pasta Salad (page 198)

Garlicky Citrus Dressing

Makes about ¾ cup

½ cup extra-virgin olive oil

6 garlic cloves

3 tablespoons fresh lemon juice

2 tablespoons spicy brown mustard

½ teaspoon kosher salt

½ teaspoon freshly ground black pepper

½ teaspoon red pepper flakes

1. In a blender or food processor, combine the olive oil, garlic, lemon juice, mustard, salt, black pepper, and pepper flakes. Blend on high until well combined, about 30 seconds. Taste for seasoning.

2. Transfer to an airtight container and store refrigerated for up to 1 week.

PUT HER TO WORK
Four Seasons Salad (page 103)

Eggs

They're the star of the show at breakfast, but, honestly, every meal is an egg-cellent time to add an egg. They make salads, roasted vegetables, and avocado toast feel a little less routine and a little more hearty. They elevate burgers, pizzas, and even pasta to the goddess tier. Read on for a shellebration of how to put a perfect egg on it every time, whatever your favorite way to cook it.

FRIED

I believe a fried egg should have a lacy, crispy white with a perfectly runny yolk. The secret to this delicate balance comes from two simple things: very hot oil and a very hot pan.

In a nonstick or cast-iron skillet, heat 2 tablespoons extra-virgin olive oil over high heat. When the oil begins to smoke, add 1 or 2 eggs to the skillet. Cook until the edges are browned and lacy, about 2 minutes, spooning hot oil from the pan onto the whites to help them cook, as needed. Season the eggs with kosher salt, freshly ground black pepper, and/or red pepper flakes, slide them out of the skillet, and serve.

BOILED

A jammy, soft-boiled egg literally oozes charisma; she's so "now." The old standby, hard-boiled, will always be there in times of need. Whichever way you like her, older is better: fresh eggs are impossible to peel, so look for a carton that's approaching expiration.

Grab a pot that's big enough to comfortably fit however many eggs you're boiling. Fill it with water and bring to a boil. When the water is boiling, use a slotted spoon to carefully add the eggs. Set a timer for 6 minutes 30 seconds for jammy eggs, or 10 minutes for hard-boiled eggs. While the eggs cook, fill a large bowl with ice water. When the timer rings, use the slotted spoon to transfer the eggs to the ice bath. Let chill until the eggs are completely cooled, about 10 minutes. Tap the wide end of the eggs against the counter to crack the shell, then carefully peel and rinse under cold water. Hard-boiled eggs can be stored in the refrigerator for up to 1 week. Otherwise, slice in half and season with kosher salt, freshly ground black pepper, and/or red pepper flakes before serving.

SCRAMBLED

One camp of people loves a splash of milk and/or half a spice drawer in their scrambled eggs. That's gorgeous if that's your fantasy, but I'm firmly a less-is-more gal when it comes to scrambling. Customize my blueprint however you like.

In a nonstick skillet (for your sanity, really use nonstick), melt 2 tablespoons unsalted butter over medium heat. While the butter melts, in a bowl, thoroughly whisk your eggs with a good pinch of kosher salt (and anything else you like), 2 or 3 eggs per person is a good rule of thumb. Pour the eggs into the melted butter and cook, undisturbed, until the edges are just set, about 30 seconds. Use a rubber spatula to drag the set edges into the center, letting the raw egg flood the skillet floor. Start to stir the eggs in a circular motion to create large curds. Remove the pan from the heat when the eggs are about 80 percent cooked—they'll finish cooking without drying out. Season with freshly ground black pepper and red pepper flakes and serve.

POACHED

The number one thing to remember about poached eggs is that even the ugly ones are delicious. These might take a little time and practice to get it just right, but can you think of a more delicious project?!

Bring a small pot of water to a gentle simmer over medium heat. While the water simmers, crack one egg into a fine-mesh strainer and let the watery membrane strain out over the sink. Transfer the strained egg to a small bowl. Using a wooden spoon, rapidly stir the simmering water to create a whirlpool. Gently pour the egg into the center of the whirlpool. Cook until the white is opaque and the edges are firm, 2 to 3 minutes. Use a slotted spoon to remove the egg, tilting the spoon to drain all the excess water. Season with kosher salt, freshly ground black pepper, and/or red pepper flakes before serving.

Eggs in Purgatory

Serves 4 to 6

6 tablespoons Herb-Infused Oil (page 31) or extra-virgin olive oil

4 cups crusty bread, cut into 2-inch cubes

3 anchovy fillets (optional)

1 pint cherry tomatoes

4 cloves Garlic Confit (see page 36), smashed, or 4 garlic cloves, thinly sliced

1 teaspoon fennel seeds

½ teaspoon freshly ground black pepper

½ teaspoon red pepper flakes

1 (28-ounce) can crushed tomatoes

1 teaspoon kosher salt

½ teaspoon dried basil

½ teaspoon dried oregano

6 large eggs

HERB SALAD

½ cup fresh mint leaves

½ cup fresh basil leaves

½ cup fresh parsley leaves

2 teaspoons drained capers, roughly chopped

1 tablespoon fresh lemon juice

1 tablespoon extra-virgin olive oil

Freshly grated Parmesan or pecorino cheese, for serving

This Italian classic sounds fairly harrowing, but, honestly, if you're gonna be stuck in purgatory, you won't find any better company than this saucy lady. Similar to shakshuka, both fresh and canned tomatoes are cooked down with a ton of spices, and a fresh herb salad tops off the whole thing. But my favorite part is the deliciously crispy chunks of bread floating around in there like drowned croutons. When you're facing the hell of making breakfast for a crowd, give them something that tastes like heaven.

1. In a large skillet, heat 4 tablespoons of the infused oil over medium heat. When the oil is shimmering, add the bread. Cook, flipping halfway through, until golden brown, 4 to 5 minutes. Transfer the croutons to a plate.

2. Add the remaining 2 tablespoons of oil to the skillet, along with the anchovies (if using), cherry tomatoes, garlic confit, fennel seeds, black pepper, and pepper flakes. Cook, stirring occasionally, until the tomatoes begin to burst, about 5 minutes. Add the crushed tomatoes, salt, dried basil, and oregano. Cook, stirring constantly, until the sauce is simmering, about 2 minutes.

3. Return the croutons to the skillet, tucking them into the tomato sauce but leaving their top halves exposed. Use a large spoon to make wells in the tomato sauce and crack the eggs into the wells. Cover the skillet and cook until the egg whites are just set but still wobbly, 6 to 8 minutes.

4. MEANWHILE, MAKE THE HERB SALAD: In a medium bowl, combine the herbs, capers, lemon juice, and olive oil and toss to coat the herbs well.

5. To serve, sprinkle the herb salad over the top of the skillet. Serve family style with a bowl of grated Parmesan alongside.

Sheet Pan Breakfast Sandwich

Serves 6 to 8

12 ounces sliced prosciutto

12 large eggs

1 cup whole milk

½ cup Fresh Mint Gremolata (page 31), Basil Almond Pesto (page 30), or store-bought pesto

1 teaspoon kosher salt

½ teaspoon freshly ground black pepper

Nonstick cooking spray

1 bunch broccoli rabe, ends trimmed

10 tablespoons whole-milk ricotta

Mom's Italian Bread (page 92) or store-bought sandwich bread, sliced, toasted, and buttered, for serving

FOR SERVING

Calabrian Chili Crisp (page 28)

Balsamic Drizzle (page 29)

BC Aioli (page 35)

Tomato Confit (page 36)

Any store-bought condiments

Note

In place of the broccoli rabe, you can sub in Broccolini, broccoli, green beans, zucchini, asparagus, spinach, chard, kale, or pretty much anything green and delicious.

Everyone loves a breakfast sandwich—that's a simple fact of life. But they can be really hard to pull off when you're feeding a crowd . . . until now! Please give a warm welcome to this very chill (okay, actually also kinda warm) sheet pan breakfast sandwich spread at your next morning party. An easy frittata gets dotted with ricotta and swirls of broccoli rabe. (So easy you can even make it ahead and serve it at room temp!) Pieces of prosciutto and slices of bread travel en masse through the oven until they're extra crispy. And from there, everyone can assemble their own dream combination, adding whatever condiments their hearts desire. Consider your crowd pleased.

1. Preheat the oven to 400°F. Line two rimmed sheet pans with parchment paper.

2. Arrange the prosciutto on the prepared sheet pans, making sure none of the pieces are touching. Bake for 8 to 10 minutes, until very crispy. Transfer to a serving platter, reserving one of the sheet pans and parchment.

3. Meanwhile, in a large bowl, combine the eggs, milk, gremolata, salt, and pepper. Whisk to mix well.

4. Spray the reserved sheet pan with nonstick spray. Pour the egg mixture evenly over the sheet. Arrange the broccoli rabe across the eggs, then dollop tablespoons of ricotta over the top.

5. Bake for 15 to 20 minutes, until the eggs are set and puffy. Remove the sheet pan from the oven and let the eggs cool for at least 10 minutes, then cut into 12 equal pieces.

6. Serve the sandwich components buffet style, with each ingredient separate, so your guests can build their sandwiches with prosciutto, toasted bread, and any combo of condiments.

Dad's Egg Salad

Serves 4

8 large hard-boiled eggs (see page 40), roughly chopped

¼ cup mayonnaise

⅔ cup pitted Castelvetrano olives, halved

1 celery stalk, thinly sliced

2 tablespoons roughly chopped fresh parsley

½ teaspoon red pepper flakes

½ teaspoon freshly ground black pepper

Kosher salt

While people love to choose sides when it comes to egg salad, I have my dad to thank for my love of the stuff. He was always making it and always adding something extra, like capers, celery . . . and sometimes even a can of tuna fish. Being very much my father's son, I love to add Castelvetrano olives to my egg salad—the briny bursts of flavor get me every time. And before you go grabbing slices of sandwich bread (or Mom's Italian Bread, page 92), I have to remind you of the old-school diner style of serving up egg salad in an adorable cup of iceberg lettuce. Could lunch get any better?

1. Place the chopped eggs in a medium bowl. Add the mayonnaise, olives, celery, parsley, pepper flakes, black pepper, and salt to taste. Stir to combine well. Taste for seasoning.

2. Tightly cover the bowl with cling wrap and refrigerate for at least 1 hour before serving, or store for up to 1 week.

Pastina: The Italian Cure-All

Serves 1

1½ cups vegetable or chicken broth

½ cup pastina

2 large eggs

¼ cup freshly grated Parmesan or pecorino cheese, plus more for serving

4 tablespoons (½ stick) unsalted butter

Freshly ground black pepper, for serving

Every Italian American kid knows that pastina is the single-most effective way to fix everything. Sick? Sad? Worst day of your life? Here's a steamy-hot bowl of pastina just for you. Every family has some variation of this dish passed through the generations, and no offense to anyone's ancestors, but my dad makes the strongest medicinal pastina I have ever had. His prescription includes the perfect combo of broth, eggs, and butter. This recipe intentionally only serves one: It's just for you, whenever you need it.

1. In a medium saucepan, bring the broth to a boil. Stir in the pastina and cook until al dente according to the package directions.

2. When the pasta is ready and has absorbed the broth, remove the pan from the heat. Crack the eggs into the pan, stirring quickly to incorporate them, then add the Parmesan and butter. Stir until the butter is completely melted.

3. Transfer the pastina to a bowl and top with more Parmesan and a few grinds of pepper. Eat up and watch all your troubles float away.

Pepper & Egg Strata

Serves 6 to 8

FILLING

3 Italian hoagie rolls, roughly cut into 2-inch pieces

3 tablespoons extra-virgin olive oil

8 ounces sliced cremini mushrooms

4 garlic cloves, thinly sliced

2 red bell peppers, sliced

1 medium white onion, halved and sliced

Kosher salt and freshly ground black pepper

2 (8-ounce) containers mozzarella pearls, drained

4 tablespoons freshly grated Parmesan cheese

Calabrian Chili Crisp (page 28) or hot sauce, for serving

CUSTARD

8 large eggs

2 tablespoons spicy brown mustard

3 cups whole milk

2 teaspoons kosher salt

1 teaspoon red pepper flakes

1 teaspoon dried oregano

Note

To make ahead, prepare through step 5, cover tightly with cling wrap, and refrigerate overnight.

The pepper-and-egg sandwich is a pillar of the Italian American experience. Roasted or grilled peppers scrambled with eggs and stuffed into a giant roll? She's a yes. My dad tells stories of eating that sandwich for breakfast every Friday during Lent when he was a kid, ready for a long Catholic school day of Mass and Communion with a belly full and happy by the grace of God (and Bimpy). This strata recipe is an homage to those iconic flavors: hunks of hoagie rolls are baked into a creamy, custardy mix of scrambled eggs, peppers, onions, mushrooms, and mozzarella. While it is indeed perfect for a Friday-morning Lenten breakfast, I also suggest making it for a lazy Sunday brunch. Amen.

1. Preheat the oven to 350°F.

2. MAKE THE FILLING: Arrange the bread on a rimmed sheet pan. Bake for about 10 minutes, until the bread is toasted and light golden brown.

3. Meanwhile, in a large skillet, heat 2 tablespoons of the olive oil over medium-high heat. When the oil is shimmering, add the mushrooms. Stir to coat in the oil, then cook undisturbed until the mushrooms are browned on the bottom, about 6 minutes. Add the remaining 1 tablespoon oil, the garlic, bell peppers, onion, and a big pinch of salt and black pepper. Cook, stirring occasionally, until the onion and bell peppers are crisp-tender, 4 to 5 minutes. Remove the skillet from the heat.

4. MAKE THE CUSTARD: In a large bowl, whisk together the eggs and mustard. Add the milk, salt, pepper flakes, and oregano. Whisk to incorporate well.

5. In a 9 x 13-inch baking dish, arrange half of the toasted bread in a single layer. Spoon half of the veggies over the bread, then add half of the mozzarella pearls and 2 tablespoons of the Parmesan. Layer on the remaining bread, pressing it down slightly into the baking dish. (But you still want some popping out of the top so it gets nice and toasted!) Add the remaining veggies over the top, then pour the custard into the baking dish. Sprinkle the remaining mozzarella pearls and 2 tablespoons Parmesan over the top.

6. Bake for 40 to 45 minutes, until the cheese is melted and golden brown. Remove the strata from the oven and let it cool for about 10 minutes in the baking dish. Slice and serve with chili crisp alongside for drizzling.

Quattro Formaggi Quiche

Serves 6 to 8

CRUST

1½ cups all-purpose flour, plus more for dusting

2 teaspoons freshly ground black pepper

1 teaspoon kosher salt

10 tablespoons unsalted butter, very cold and cut into pieces

3 to 4 tablespoons ice water

FILLING

6 large eggs

1 cup heavy cream

½ cup shredded mozzarella cheese

½ cup freshly grated Parmesan cheese

½ cup crumbled Gorgonzola cheese

½ cup whole-milk ricotta cheese

1 tablespoon thinly sliced chives

1 teaspoon kosher salt

½ teaspoon red pepper flakes

In her early twenties, my mom was a waitress at a restaurant called The Pie Plate in Waterbury, Connecticut, and they were famous for their quiche. She somehow got her hands on the recipe and started making endless variations of fillings and styles. So I grew up in a quiche-heavy household, and her enthusiasm encouraged me to be quiche-curious later in life. The classic quattro formaggi pizza is the inspiration here, with mozzarella, Parmesan, Gorgonzola, and ricotta folded together with eggs and cream, all cradled by an extra-peppery crust.

1. MAKE THE CRUST: In a food processor, combine the flour, black pepper, and salt. Pulse 2 times to mix everything together. Add the butter (make sure it's very cold!) and pulse 4 or 5 times to break it into pea-size pieces. Add 2 tablespoons of the ice water. With the motor running, gradually add more ice water, 1 tablespoon at a time, until a dough begins to form.

2. Turn the dough out onto a piece of parchment paper and press into a thick disk. Wrap the dough in the parchment and refrigerate for at least 1 hour or overnight.

3. Preheat the oven to 350°F.

4. Lightly flour a clean work surface and set the dough in the center. Dust the top of the dough with flour, then, using a rolling pin, roll out the dough into a large circle, about 14 inches across and ¼-inch thick, adding more flour as needed to prevent sticking. Fold the dough in half in one direction, then in half again in the other direction. Transfer the dough to a 9-inch pie plate with the corner of the dough in the center of the plate. Unfold the dough, lifting and adjusting as needed to cover the plate.

recipe continues

5. Trim the excess dough from the edges and crimp the dough into whatever shape you like. Use a fork to poke holes along the bottom and sides of the dough. Place a piece of parchment paper in the pie plate and add pie weights, dried beans, or coffee beans on top. Bake for about 30 minutes, until the crust is lightly golden brown. (Fun fact: This is called par-baking!)

6. MEANWHILE, MAKE THE FILLING: In a large bowl, whisk the eggs. Add the cream, mozzarella, Parmesan, Gorgonzola, ricotta, chives, salt, and pepper flakes. Whisk again just to combine.

7. Remove the crust from the oven and carefully lift the parchment and weights out of the crust. Reduce the temperature to 300°F.

8. Pour the filling into the crust and return it to the oven. Bake for about 1 hour, until the filling is puffy and mostly set with the slightest wobble. Remove the quiche and let it cool for 1 hour before slicing and serving.

Salami & Egg Sheet Pan Hash

Serves 6 to 8

HASH

4 tablespoons extra-virgin olive oil

2 pounds russet potatoes, peeled and shredded, or 1 (30-ounce) bag frozen shredded potatoes

2 (3-ounce) packages sliced hard salami

2 tablespoons freshly grated Parmesan cheese

1 teaspoon kosher salt

½ teaspoon freshly ground black pepper

½ teaspoon onion powder

½ teaspoon garlic powder

½ teaspoon fennel seeds

½ teaspoon red pepper flakes

6 to 8 large eggs

RADICCHIO SALAD

1 tablespoon honey

1 tablespoon spicy brown mustard

1 tablespoon red wine vinegar

1 tablespoon extra-virgin olive oil

½ medium head radicchio, thinly sliced

Note

To prevent the potatoes from turning brown, shred them into a large bowl of cold water with a squeeze of lemon juice. You can even tightly cover the bowl with cling wrap and refrigerate overnight if you like. Just be sure to rinse the potatoes before using.

This one goes out to my fellow crispy, crunchy girls. It's filled with so many things I love: toasty shredded hash browns, golden and greasy salami, perfectly baked eggs, and a sweet and tangy salad. Not to mention, she's a sheet pan meal, so cleanup is easy-peasy. This dish pays its respects to one of my favorite Italian breakfast combos, salami and eggs, typically enjoyed in sandwich form. I swear it will have you saying, "Bacon and eggs? Never heard of her . . ." as soon as you take your first bite.

1. MAKE THE HASH: Preheat the oven to 400°F with the racks set in the upper and lower thirds. Rub 2 tablespoons of the olive oil over a rimmed sheet pan.

2. Rinse the potatoes under cold water to remove excess starch. Drain well, then spread over a clean kitchen towel. Tightly roll up the towel and press firmly to remove excess water from the potatoes. Place the potatoes in a large bowl.

3. Stack the salami on a cutting board and cut into ¼-inch-wide strips. Add the salami to the bowl with the potatoes, along with the Parmesan, salt, black pepper, onion powder, garlic powder, fennel seeds, pepper flakes, and the remaining 2 tablespoons olive oil. Use clean hands to toss everything together, making sure the potatoes are well coated.

4. Spread the potato-and-salami mixture in a single layer on the prepared sheet pan. Bake on the lower rack for 15 to 20 minutes, until the bottom of the potatoes start getting crispy. Transfer the sheet pan to the top rack and bake for another 10 to 15 minutes, until the potatoes are browned and crispy on top.

5. MEANWHILE, MAKE THE RADICCHIO SALAD: In a medium bowl, whisk together the honey, mustard, vinegar, and olive oil to combine. Add the sliced radicchio and toss to coat. Set aside to marinate.

6. When the hash is browned, crack 6 to 8 eggs (depending on how many people you're serving) on top of the hash. Return the sheet pan to the top rack of the oven for about 5 minutes more, until the egg whites are set but the yolks are still runny.

7. Sprinkle the radicchio salad over the hash. Serve directly from the sheet pan, using a spatula to slice into squares, making sure everyone gets an egg.

Leftover Pasta Frittata

Serves 2 to 4

6 large eggs

2 tablespoons freshly grated Parmesan or pecorino cheese, plus more for serving

½ teaspoon freshly ground black pepper

¼ teaspoon kosher salt

¼ teaspoon red pepper flakes

1 tablespoon extra-virgin olive oil

1 cup cooked pasta, such as spaghetti, fettuccine, or bucatini

On the rare occasion I have leftover pasta after dinner—very, *very* rare—this frittata makes for a special treat the next morning. Bimpy taught me about this delight when I was young. It didn't matter what kind of pasta shape, what sort of sauce, or what time of day it was—he always made me feel like the world had stopped and it was just the two of us making magic together. Adult Grossy, in his typical way, likes to be sure the pasta gets extra crispy on the bottom of the pan, the eggs are extra fluffy and cheesy, and the frittata is served straight out of the skillet. This recipe is for 1 cup of pasta, but you can adjust the number of eggs up or down to meet whatever you have on hand.

1. Turn the broiler on high.

2. In a medium bowl, combine the eggs, Parmesan, black pepper, salt, and pepper flakes. Whisk thoroughly to combine.

3. In a medium oven-safe skillet, heat the olive oil over medium heat. When the oil is shimmering, add the pasta. Cook, stirring occasionally, until heated through, about 3 minutes. Pour in the egg mixture and tilt the skillet to distribute evenly. Cook, undisturbed, until the edges of the eggs are fully cooked and beginning to pull away from the sides of the skillet, about 5 minutes.

4. Transfer the skillet to the oven and broil for about 3 minutes, until the eggs are set and the frittata is slightly puffy. Cut into quarters, sprinkle with Parmesan, and serve.

Spinach & Mushroom Baked Eggs

Serves 2

1 tablespoon unsalted butter

1 cup sliced mushrooms, such as baby bella or shiitake

2 cups packed fresh spinach

Kosher salt and freshly ground black pepper

2 large eggs

4 tablespoons heavy cream

FOR SERVING

Red pepper flakes

Chopped fresh parsley

Calabrian Chili Crisp (page 28)

Slices of Mom's Italian Bread (page 92), toasted

Note

6-ounce ramekins also work great (just adjust to 1 tablespoon of cream in each ramekin), as do small skillets made for individual servings! And, of course, you can multiply the ingredients to serve 4, 6, 8, and so on.

I am sorry, but *what* is cuter than little ramekins or mini skillets with creamy eggs baked into them? So small, so dainty . . . so the opposite of everything I stand for. I fondly remember my first time eating a baked egg with a toasted baguette cut on an angle, meant for dipping. When I grabbed my toast, my pinky automatically stood straight up in the air because I am a lady. I swirled everything together, took a bite, and immediately dropped a large blob of yolk onto my shirt. *Ecstasy*, I thought. My sincere hope is that you feel the same way about these baked eggs. Pinkies up!

1. In a large skillet, melt the butter over medium-high heat. Add the mushrooms and cook, stirring occasionally, until golden brown, about 5 minutes. Add the spinach and cook, stirring, until wilted, about 2 minutes. Season with salt and black pepper. Divide the veggies evenly between two 8-ounce ramekins. Set the ramekins on a quarter sheet pan.

2. Crack 1 egg into each ramekin, then pour 2 tablespoons of the cream over the top of each. Bake for 10 to 12 minutes, until the egg whites are opaque but the yolks are still soft.

3. Remove the sheet pan from the oven. Sprinkle each ramekin with a pinch each of pepper flakes and parsley, and finish them with a drizzle of chili crisp. Serve with toast alongside for dipping.

Uncle Phil's Deviled Eggs

Makes 24 eggs

12 large hard-boiled eggs (see page 40), peeled and rinsed

6 tablespoons Giardiniera brine (page 32, or from a store-bought jar), plus pieces of Giardiniera to garnish

2 tablespoons mayonnaise

½ teaspoon smoked paprika

Kosher salt

My uncle Phil was not known for his cooking—he lived with Bimpy, so you can't blame him for not bothering to learn. But he was famous for showing up to every single party with a tray of deviled eggs, proudly telling anyone who would listen that he made them himself. His special touch was topping them with halved olives for some extra flair. In my version, I embrace the many pickled vegetables in a jar of giardiniera for that special hit of beautiful brininess. I also add a bit of the giardiniera brine into the yolk mixtures, which brings a level of drama that I'm positive would make Uncle Phil proud.

1. On a large cutting board, halve each egg lengthwise. Remove the yolks, dropping them into a medium bowl. Reserve the egg white halves on the board. To the yolks, add the giardiniera brine and mayonnaise. Season with the paprika and a pinch of salt. Use a fork to mash and stir until a smooth filling forms. Taste for seasoning.

2. Transfer the mixture into a small zip-top bag. Snip a corner off the bottom of the bag, and twist the top of the bag to remove the air and push the mixture down to the snipped corner. Press the filling out through the slit and pipe it into the reserved egg white halves.

3. Transfer the filled eggs to a serving platter and top with pieces of giardiniera. Serve immediately or refrigerate for up to 4 hours, so you have plenty of time to do your hair and makeup for the party.

Appetizers

Truly nothing compares to a salty, greasy, crispy bite of fried food. While frying at home might feel intimidating, it's really all about getting set up for success. Frying is a time for undivided attention, so you want to be sure you have everything at hand before even turning on the burner. Follow these tips, and fry day will be fry yay every time.

READY

THE ROOM

Open the windows and get the exhaust fan going. Give the kids and pets something to distract them and warn everyone else to steer clear while frying is underway.

SET UP FOR SUCCESS

It may be counterintuitive, but think about how frying ends before you even start. Line a sheet pan or plate with plenty of paper towels for draining the fried food. Set salt or any other finishing seasoning nearby for quick access—you always want to season fried food while it's screaming hot. While you're at it, set out your tongs, strainer, and any other utensils.

Get Hot

As for the type of pot you should use, a Dutch oven or a large, heavy saucepan are ideal for heat retention and room to fry. But the most essential tool is a deep-fry thermometer. Clip it to the lip of the pot, and you'll easily be able to monitor the oil temp.Be sure you're at the right temp before anything hits the oil, adjusting the burner's heat up or down to keep it steady. If you're working in batches, you may need to check the thermometer in between, as the oil temp will fluctuate.

DRAG HER

Arrange any batters, crumbs, flour, or eggs ahead of time so you can dredge in a smooth, organized way. Use one hand for dry dipping and one hand for wet dipping to avoid gummy fingers. Most importantly, release your expectations of perfection; you don't have to cover every inch of food. Sometimes a peek of the food under a craggy batter is even more beautiful than full coverage.

Play It Safe

Use heat-safe tongs to add food to and remove it from the oil, keeping your hand and arm a safe distance from the action. Always lower food into the hot oil slowly and gently to avoid splashes. A spider strainer is also a great tool for scooping out a bunch of stuff at the same time.

TAKE

Rushing through the frying process will only cause a major headache—and soggy food. Fry in small batches so your food has plenty of room to brown evenly. Check it often to be sure you're hitting the sweet spot of crispy and golden brown.

YOUR TIME

It Doesn't Get Batter Than This

Makes 2 cups

1 cup all-purpose flour

⅔ cup freshly grated Parmesan or Pecorino cheese

1½ cups seltzer

When it comes to a light and crispy batter that's perfect for pretty much anything, I whip up this simple three-ingredient standby. It's airy, delicate, and just the right amount of salty.

In a medium bowl, whisk together the flour and Parmesan. Pour in the seltzer and whisk until incorporated into a slightly lumpy batter.

Fried Calamari & Pepperoncini

Serves 8

2 quarts vegetable oil, for frying

It Doesn't Get Batter Than This
(page 67)

2 pounds whole calamari, cut into
¼-inch-thick rings, or calamari rings
and tentacles, thawed if frozen

1 (12-ounce) jar pepperoncini rings,
drained

Kosher salt

FOR SERVING
Lemon wedges

AP Aioli (page 35)

Grossy's Marinara (page 153) or
store-bought marinara sauce

On the rare occasion when my family dined out, we went to
Nino's in Waterbury, Connecticut. (Of course, we ate Italian
American because we liked to be comfy even out of the house.)
The first dish to hit the table was always fried calamari, and it
was placed directly in front of Bimpy. The second dish to hit the
table was always another order of calamari, and it was placed
in the center for sharing. What made Nino's so special were the
rings of pepperoncini scattered in with the calamari, adding a
perfect bite of tang. This recipe is my ode to that classic app,
which, in my opinion, is how calamari should always be served.

1. Clip a deep-fry thermometer to the side of a Dutch oven and set it
over medium heat. Add the vegetable oil and heat it to 375°F.

2. Meanwhile, pour the batter into a rimmed quarter sheet pan or 9
x 13-inch baking dish. Pat the calamari and pepperoncini with paper
towels to dry thoroughly. Separate the rings, tentacles (if using), and
pepperoncini. Use tongs to toss a quarter of the calamari rings into
the batter, turning to coat.

3. Holding the sheet pan close to the stove, use the tongs to remove
the calamari from the batter, allowing any excess to drip off, then
carefully lower them into the oil. Cook until the batter is golden
brown and crisp, 4 to 5 minutes. Use a spider strainer to transfer the
rings to paper towels to drain. Immediately season with a pinch of
salt. Continue frying the rings in batches, allowing the oil to return to
375°F between each batch.

4. When all the rings are fried, repeat the process with the tentacles
(if using).

5. Use a spider strainer to lower a third of the pepperoncini rings
into the oil (do not batter them). Step back—no matter how dry those
pepperoncini were, they will still have some fight left in them; don't
panic when the oil starts sputtering. Fry until the pepperoncini are
golden brown and slightly crisp, 3 to 5 minutes, then transfer to
paper towels to drain and season with a pinch of salt.

6. Pile the fried rings, tentacles (if using), and pepperoncini onto
a platter. Serve with plenty of lemon wedges and aioli, marinara,
or both.

Fried Stuffed Olives

Serves 8

1 (5.5-ounce) jar pitted Castelvetrano olives, drained

4 ounces Fontina cheese, cut into ½-inch cubes

1 pound hot Italian sausage, casings removed

2 quarts vegetable oil, for frying

¼ cup all-purpose flour

It Doesn't Get Batter Than This (page 67)

Stuffing an olive with sausage, coating it in breadcrumbs, and then deep frying it until golden seems like it should be illegal, but, in fact, this practice has a long history as an antipasti. (Italians: We're extra in everything we do.) The official name for this dish is *olive all'ascolana*, and you might even find it on the menu at your favorite red sauce spot. I am always one to try to re-create a restaurant dish at home (I get it from my mother), but in this case, I think I took two left turns and ended up striking gold. Instead of sausage stuffing, I prefer the sharpness of Fontina cheese—but the sausage becomes a snuggly blanket for the outside of the olive. And forget breadcrumbs; we're going full tilt by bathing these in the perfect batter for a crunchy crust that shatters when you bite into it. By the time you get to the melty, cheesy core, you will be whispering "olive you." Olive you, too.

1. Pat the olives dry with paper towels. Stuff each olive with cheese (overflow is both okay and encouraged). Use about 2 tablespoons of sausage to cover each olive completely, forming a little meatball.

2. Clip a deep-fry thermometer to the side of a large Dutch oven and set it over medium heat. Add the vegetable oil and heat it to 375°F.

3. Meanwhile, place the flour in a medium bowl and pour the batter into a large bowl. Use tongs to toss a quarter of the balls in the flour, turning to coat, then transfer them to the batter, doing the same.

4. Holding the bowl close to the stove, use the tongs to remove the balls from the batter, allowing any excess to drip off, then carefully lower them into the oil. Cook until the batter is golden brown and crisp, 5 to 6 minutes. Use a spider strainer to transfer the balls to paper towels to drain. Continue frying the balls in batches, allowing the oil to return to 375°F between each batch.

5. Arrange the fried olives on a platter and serve.

Fried Stuffed Squash Blossoms

Serves 8

1 cup whole-milk ricotta cheese

1 egg yolk

¼ cup finely chopped fresh mint

⅓ cup freshly grated Parmesan or pecorino cheese

Kosher salt and freshly ground black pepper

Red pepper flakes

12 squash blossoms, stamens removed

2 quarts vegetable oil, for frying

It Doesn't Get Batter Than This (page 67)

The most underrated veggie, in my opinion, is the squash blossom. It's not that she's disliked—she's just not well known. If you're, in fact, not familiar, allow me to enlighten you: Squash blossoms are the edible flowers grown from a squash plant, sometimes called zucchini flowers. You can typically find them from late spring through the early fall, and, throughout my childhood, Bimpy and Grandma Katherine would harvest them from their garden to make little fritters that I still dream about. My recipe is a version of theirs, but I stuff the blossoms with cheese before frying to add extra richness . . . and maybe a little bit of drama.

1. In a large bowl, combine the ricotta, egg yolk, mint, Parmesan, and big pinches of salt, black pepper, and pepper flakes. Stir to combine thoroughly, then scoop the mixture into a large zip-top bag. Snip a corner off the bottom of the bag, and twist the top of the bag to remove the air and push the mixture down to the bottom.

2. Carefully pry open a squash blossom and hold it open with one hand. With your other hand, gently squeeze the bag to fill the blossom with the ricotta mixture. (This process won't be perfect—just get the job done as best as you can and remember to laugh.) Twist the top of the blossom to seal the filling inside. Repeat with the rest of the blossoms.

3. Clip a deep-fry thermometer to the side of a Dutch oven and set it over medium heat. Add the vegetable oil and heat it to 375°F.

4. Meanwhile, pour the batter into a rimmed quarter sheet pan or 9 x 13-inch baking dish. Use tongs to toss a quarter of the stuffed blossoms in the batter, turning to coat.

5. Holding the sheet pan close to the stove, use the tongs to remove the blossoms from the batter, allowing any excess to drip off, then carefully lower them into the oil. Cook until the batter is golden brown and crisp, 5 to 6 minutes. Use a spider strainer to transfer the blossoms to paper towels to drain. Immediately season with a pinch of salt. Continue frying the blossoms in batches, allowing the oil to return to 375°F between each batch.

6. Arrange the fried blossoms on a platter and serve.

Fritto Misto

Serves 8

2 quarts vegetable oil, for frying

It Doesn't Get Batter Than This
(page 67)

4 pounds mixed vegetables, trimmed
and sliced as needed

Kosher salt

AP Aioli (page 35) or store-bought
aioli, for serving

Everyone is always talking about eating their vegetables, and according to me, this is the very best way to do it. You see, I like my vegetables to be crispy crisp, and there is nothing crispier than a fritto misto! It's the perfect appetizer for a crowd, not only because it's an abundant and impressive platter of food, but also because you get to watch your friends and family fight over their favorites in the pile. But once the turf wars die down, the only noise you will hear is crunching, which is the best compliment any chef could hope for. This recipe works with any veggies, but some of my favorites for the occasion are acorn squash, broccoli or Broccolini, cauliflower, fennel, green beans, onions, zucchini, or even thinly sliced lemon.

1. Clip a deep-fry thermometer to the side of a large Dutch oven and set it over medium heat. Add the vegetable oil and heat it to 375°F.

2. Meanwhile, pour the batter into a rimmed quarter sheet pan or 9 x 13-inch baking dish. Use tongs to toss a quarter of the vegetables in the batter, turning to coat.

3. Holding the sheet pan close to the stove, use the tongs to remove the veggies from the batter, allowing any excess to drip off, then carefully lower them into the oil. Cook until the batter is golden brown and crisp, 5 to 6 minutes. Use a spider strainer to transfer the veggies to paper towels to drain. Immediately season with a pinch of salt. Continue frying the veggies in batches, allowing the oil to return to 375°F between each batch.

4. Arrange the fried veggies on a platter. Serve with aioli alongside for dipping.

Mozzarella en Carrozza

Makes 10 skewers

ANCHOVY BUTTER

½ cup (1 stick) unsalted butter

3 anchovy fillets

1 teaspoon minced fresh parsley

SKEWERS

16 ounces fresh mozzarella (vacuum-sealed without water)

1 Italian hoagie roll

2 quarts vegetable oil, for frying

10 (8-inch) wooden skewers

It Doesn't Get Batter Than This (page 67)

Certain things I've eaten throughout my life are so delicious, so memorable, and so satisfying that I know I will never forget them. The mozzarella en carrozza at Pizzeria Delfina in San Francisco is one of those core memories. Instead of the traditional version (kind of an Italian grilled cheese), Delfina blew my mind with a skewer of alternating mozzarella and bread chunks, fried in a batter until super crispy, and bathed in anchovy butter. We can't go back in time, but this recipe takes me as close to that first bite at Delfina as I can get. I hope this version becomes a core memory in your heart, too.

1. MAKE THE ANCHOVY BUTTER: In a small skillet, melt the butter over low heat. Add the anchovies and cook, smashing and stirring, until the fillets are dissolved, about 3 minutes. Remove the pan from the heat and stir in the parsley.

2. MAKE THE SKEWERS: Cut the mozzarella into about eight 1-inch-thick rounds, then cut each round in quarters. Cut the hoagie roll in the same way to create equal-size pieces.

3. Clip a deep-fry thermometer to the side of a large Dutch oven and set it over medium heat. Add the oil and heat it to 375°F.

4. MEANWHILE, SKEWER THE MOZZARELLA AND BREAD IN THIS PATTERN: mozz, bread, mozz, bread, mozz. Keep the ingredients tight toward the pointy end of the skewer for easy dipping and frying. You'll have enough to make 10 skewers with some extra pieces in case anything falls apart (and for a chef's snack).

5. Pour the batter into a quart jar or large, tall glass. Dip a skewer into the batter, tilting the jar as needed to cover the bread and cheese.

6. Slide the skewer into the oil, resting the blunt end of the skewer on the edge of the Dutch oven. Repeat with another 2 or 3 skewers, enough to fill the pot without overcrowding it. Cook, using the ends of the sticks to rotate halfway through, until the coating is deep golden brown and the mozz is oozing, 5 to 6 minutes. Transfer the skewers to paper towels to drain. Continue frying the skewers in batches, allowing the oil to return to 375°F between each batch.

7. While the last skewers are frying, return the anchovy butter to low heat to warm it through for a minute or two. Arrange the skewers on a platter and spoon the warm anchovy butter over the fried mozz before serving.

Baked Brie Bread Bowl

Serves 4 to 6

1 (8-ounce) Brie wheel

1 large sourdough boule

4 tablespoons (½ stick) unsalted butter, melted

2 tablespoons freshly grated Parmesan or pecorino cheese

1 tablespoon fresh thyme leaves

2 tablespoons Mostarda di Frutta (page 34) or store-bought fig jam

My sister Diana's official title is Queen of Baked Brie. For years—even decades—she has been smothering Brie with jam and wrapping it in phyllo for every family gathering. The dish is Peak Pinterest Mom, and if I had to describe Queen Diana, the phrase I'd use would be, well, "Peak Pinterest Mom." Influenced by her, I have been known to dabble in baked Brie (and my own Pinterest Mom aesthetic) as well, and this version might just be my most exciting creation. Crusty bread, ready to pull and dip (it's like the bend and snap, but for snacks) into a well of warm, gooey Brie and sweet mostarda di frutta—though you can use any jam you like—sprinkled with fresh thyme leaves and a bit of grated cheese. Your guests won't be able to "pin" this recipe fast enough!

1. Preheat the oven to 350°F. Line a rimmed quarter sheet pan with foil.

2. Slice off the top rind of the Brie wheel just enough to expose the cheese. Slice off the top inch of the sourdough boule to create a flat surface. Center the Brie wheel on top of the loaf and cut around it, careful to cut all the way down to, but not through, the bottom crust of the boule. Remove the Brie from the loaf and remove the center section of the boule. Slice the remaining outer crust of the bread bowl straight down in 1-inch segments, cutting all the way down, but not through, the bottom crust. Cut the reserved bread scraps into 1-inch croutons.

3. Place the croutons on the prepared sheet pan and toss with 1 tablespoon of the melted butter and 1 tablespoon of the Parmesan. Nestle the bread bowl in the center of the sheet pan and arrange the croutons around it. Brush the inside and rim of the bowl with the remaining 3 tablespoons melted butter. Return the Brie wheel to the center of the bowl. Sprinkle the remaining 1 tablespoon Parmesan and the thyme leaves around the rim of the bowl. Spoon the Mostarda di Frutta over the top of the Brie wheel.

4. Bake for 20 to 30 minutes, until the Brie is gooey and the bread is toasted. Transfer the bowl and croutons to a platter and serve.

Bruschetta Dip

Serves 8

TOAST

1 baguette, thinly sliced

Extra-virgin olive oil

1 garlic clove

DIP

1½ pounds Roma tomatoes

2 garlic cloves, grated

2 tablespoons extra-virgin olive oil

1 tablespoon red wine vinegar

1 bunch fresh basil leaves, roughly chopped

Kosher salt and freshly ground black pepper

1 (5.3-ounce) container Greek yogurt

I grew up a Food Network kid, which means that when I close my eyes, I can vividly hear Giada De Laurentiis saying the word *bruschetta* with the most excited yell about halfway through the word. Her pronunciation was truly chaotic, yet we thrived on it. In this era, one in which we might pronounce *bruschetta* with softer tones, we're laying this traditional topping on a bed of yogurt and surrounding her with plenty of toasty bread for dipping. A simple blend of oil, vinegar, garlic, and basil make for a dip that's refreshing, light, cool, creamy, and oh so summery.

1. MAKE THE TOAST: Preheat the oven to 450°F. Line a rimmed sheet pan with parchment paper.

2. Arrange the baguette slices on the prepared sheet pan. Drizzle them with olive oil, then bake for about 8 minutes, until crisp and golden brown. Remove the sheet pan from the oven and gently rub each slice with the garlic clove.

3. MEANWHILE, MAKE THE DIP: Halve the tomatoes and discard the seeds and cores. Roughly chop the tomatoes into ¼-inch pieces and place them in a medium bowl. Add the garlic, olive oil, vinegar, basil, and a big pinch each of salt and pepper. Stir to mix, then let the tomatoes marinate at room temperature for 30 minutes.

4. Drain the tomatoes, reserving both the solids and the liquid. In a medium bowl, combine 3 tablespoons of the reserved liquid, the Greek yogurt, and a big pinch each of salt and pepper. Stir to combine well, then taste for seasoning.

5. Swoop the yogurt over the bottom of a platter, then spoon the reserved tomatoes over the top. Serve with the toasts alongside for dipping.

Caponata Toast

Serves 8

CAPONATA

2 tablespoons extra-virgin olive oil

2 celery stalks, thinly sliced

1 large white onion, diced

4 garlic cloves, thinly sliced

Kosher salt

1 large eggplant (1½ to 2 pounds), cut into 1-inch pieces

1 (14-ounce) can crushed tomatoes

½ cup drained capers (from a 3.5-ounce jar)

½ cup pitted Castelvetrano olives, roughly chopped

2 tablespoons red wine vinegar

2 tablespoons honey

Red pepper flakes

Eggplant is at the core of the Italian American experience. We always had an abundance of it in my family's gardens, and I loved watching them grow and mature throughout the summer. (This may be why I am gay? Who knows.) One of my favorite ways to use eggplant is to make caponata with it, an Italian word that basically translates to "flavor boost." The combination of capers and olives with a touch of both vinegar and honey provides huge depth to cut through the rich eggplant. The topping is versatile and can be used on so many things (think: a pile of pasta), but spreading it over toast that's already slathered with ricotta is one of my great joys.

1. MAKE THE CAPONATA: In a large saucepan, heat the olive oil over medium heat. When the oil is shimmering, add the celery, onion, garlic, and a good pinch of salt. Cook, stirring occasionally, until the onion begins to turn translucent, about 8 minutes. Stir in the eggplant and add 2 tablespoons water. Cover and simmer for about 10 minutes, checking halfway and adding more water as needed to keep the saucepan from drying out, until the eggplant is beginning to soften. Add the crushed tomatoes and another generous pinch of salt. Simmer, uncovered, stirring occasionally, until the eggplant is falling apart and the sauce is thick, about 10 minutes more.

2. Remove the pan from the heat and stir in the capers, olives, vinegar, honey, and a pinch of pepper flakes. Taste for seasoning. Transfer the mixture to a medium bowl, cover tightly with cling wrap, and refrigerate for at least 1 hour or preferably overnight for maximum flavor.

3. MAKE THE TOAST: When you're ready to serve, in a medium bowl, stir together the ricotta, black pepper, and a big pinch of salt. In a separate medium bowl, combine the celery, basil, mint, parsley, almonds, and lemon juice. Toss to mix well.

4. In a large skillet, heat the olive oil over medium heat. When the oil is shimmering, add 4 slices of bread (or however many will fit comfortably) and cook until nicely toasted, about 2 minutes per side. Transfer the toasted slices to a platter and sprinkle the top of each slice with a tiny pinch of salt. Repeat with the remaining bread, adding more oil to the skillet as needed.

TOAST

1 (15-ounce) container whole-milk ricotta

1 tablespoon freshly ground black pepper

Kosher salt

1 celery stalk, thinly sliced

½ cup roughly chopped fresh basil

½ cup roughly chopped fresh mint

½ cup whole fresh parsley

½ cup roughly chopped roasted almonds

Juice of ½ lemon

2 tablespoons extra-virgin olive oil, plus more as needed

8 thick slices crusty bread or Mom's Italian Bread (page 92)

5. Divide the ricotta mixture among the toasted bread (about 3 tablespoons per slice) and smear it in gorgeous waves. Spoon the caponata over the top (about ½ cup per slice). Garnish each toast with the herby almond mixture and serve.

Italian Gay Wedding Soup

Serves 8

SOUP

2 tablespoons extra-virgin olive oil

1 large red onion, diced

2 celery stalks, diced

2 medium carrots, diced

2 garlic cloves, grated

Kosher salt and freshly ground black pepper

2 quarts chicken broth

1 Parmesan rind

1 bunch rainbow chard, stems and leaves roughly chopped

Freshly grated Parmesan cheese, for serving

MEATBALLS

1 pound chicken sausage, casings removed

1 garlic clove, grated

1 teaspoon dried oregano

½ teaspoon red pepper flakes

½ teaspoon smoked paprika

Note
Instead of tossing your ground-down Parmesan rinds into the trash, chuck them into a zip-top bag and stow them in the freezer until it's time to plunk them into your soup. A Parmesan rind brings a ton of savory, salty flavor to any soup!

Italian wedding soup, one of the most classic comfort foods, does not get its name because it is served at Italian weddings. The name comes from the Italian phrase *minestra maritata* ("married soup") because of the flavor that comes from the marriage of the tastiest little meatballs to the freshest greens, which are traditionally escarole, spinach, or kale. With chicken sausage and rainbow chard, along with a medley of other bright veggies, this iconic dish gets a fresh and fun makeover. Best of all, the swirl of color also says, "Gay Pride!" so love wins. If you can't find rainbow chard, any other hearty green will do, but your soup won't be, well, gay.

1. MAKE THE SOUP: In a Dutch oven, heat the olive oil over medium heat. When the oil is shimmering, add the onion, celery, carrots, and garlic, and season with salt and black pepper. Cook, stirring occasionally, until the vegetables are vibrant in color and the onion is just beginning to soften, about 3 minutes. Add the chicken broth and Parmesan rind. Bring the soup to a simmer, then taste for seasoning.

2. MEANWHILE, MAKE THE MEATBALLS: In a medium bowl, combine the chicken sausage, garlic, oregano, pepper flakes, and paprika. Mix to combine well.

3. When the soup is simmering, use a soup spoon to scoop up small portions of the meat mixture, using a second soup spoon to drop it directly into the soup. (The meatballs can be any size as you like. They will be messy and misshapen, and that is exactly the point.) Continue simmering until the meatballs are cooked through, about 5 minutes more. Stir in the rainbow chard until the leaves are just beginning to wilt, about 3 minutes.

4. Remove the pot from the heat and discard the Parmesan rind. Ladle the soup into bowls and serve with plenty of grated Parmesan.

Marinated Tomato Toast

Serves 4

TOMATOES

2 large heirloom tomatoes, cut into 8 thick slices

4 garlic cloves

Juice of 1 lemon

2 tablespoons extra-virgin olive oil

Flaky sea salt and freshly ground black pepper

TOAST

2 tablespoons extra-virgin olive oil, plus more as needed

4 thick slices crusty bread or Mom's Italian Bread (page 92)

Kosher salt

4 (2-ounce) or 2 (4-ounce) burrata balls

FOR SERVING

Red pepper flakes

Finely chopped fresh basil

Balsamic Drizzle (page 29) or store-bought balsamic glaze, for serving

Is anything better than a *perfect* tomato? When tomato season hits, it's all I can do to not eat them 24/7, often on toast, sometimes with mayo, other times with cottage cheese or cream cheese or ricotta. Oh, and definitely with burrata. *Perfect* may be tough to achieve, but I come from a family that does not believe in *bad* tomatoes—everything the garden gave us was at least *good*, and we used it all. The trick to making even the imperfect ones sing is to marinate them in olive oil, salt, garlic, and lemon juice. Piled on fried toast, oozing with cheese, and maybe even a little balsamic drizzle . . . it's not just *good*—it's *great*.

1. MAKE THE TOMATOES: Arrange the tomato slices on a large plate or quarter sheet pan. Grate the garlic cloves directly over the top of each slice. Squeeze on the lemon juice, then drizzle with the olive oil. Season generously with flaky salt and black pepper. Set aside to marinate at room temperature for at least 15 minutes or up to 1 hour.

2. MAKE THE TOAST: In a large skillet, heat the olive oil over medium heat. When the oil is shimmering, add the bread (however many slices will fit comfortably—work in batches if needed) and cook until nicely toasted, about 2 minutes per side. Transfer the toasted slices to a platter and sprinkle the top of each slice with a tiny pinch of kosher salt.

3. Break and evenly divide the burrata directly on top of the toast. Add two tomato slices to each piece.

4. Finish the toast with pepper flakes, basil, and a drizzle of balsamic glaze before serving.

Ribollita

Serves 4 to 6

4 tablespoons extra-virgin olive oil, plus more as needed

4 to 5 cups torn crusty bread (1-inch cubes)

1 large white onion, diced

6 garlic cloves, thinly sliced

2 rosemary sprigs

Kosher salt and freshly ground black pepper

1 Parmesan rind

4 cups vegetable or chicken broth

1 (28-ounce) can crushed tomatoes

1 bunch lacinato kale, woody stems discarded and leaves sliced into ribbons

Freshly grated Parmesan or pecorino cheese, for serving

Maybe because my family insisted that we eat at the same two restaurants over and over, I have found that as an adult, I am quite the creature of habit. Nothing beats walking into a restaurant, being greeted by everyone there, and knowing everything will be delicious. When I lived in San Francisco, my spot was the now-closed Bar Jules. Everything on the menu was a testament to simplicity, and the ribollita soup was one of my go-tos. I was in awe of how a few simple ingredients—tomatoes, herbs, hunks of bread—could be so perfect. This recipe strives for that same level, letting the ingredients speak for themselves. It's warm, comforting, and the kind of low-effort, high-reward recipe I love the most.

1. In a Dutch oven, heat 2 tablespoons of the olive oil over medium heat. When the oil is shimmering, working in batches as needed, add the bread cubes and cook, stirring, until golden brown all over, about 6 minutes total. Transfer the croutons to a plate.

2. Add the remaining 2 tablespoons olive oil to the pot. When the oil is shimmering, add the onion, garlic, and rosemary and season with salt and pepper. Cook, stirring occasionally, until the onion is soft and translucent, about 8 minutes. Add the Parmesan rind, broth, and crushed tomatoes. Season again with salt and pepper. Bring the soup to a simmer, cover, and reduce the heat to low. Cook for about 10 minutes, until the flavors are melded.

3. Remove the pot from the heat, uncover, and stir in the kale to wilt, about 5 minutes. Divide the croutons among bowls and ladle the soup over the top. Sprinkle with plenty of Parmesan and serve.

MOM'S ITALIAN BREAD, PAGE 92

Mom's Italian Bread

Makes 2 loaves or 9 dinner rolls or 8 breadsticks or a combo of everything

1 (¼-ounce) packet active dry yeast

3 tablespoons sugar

3 tablespoons extra-virgin olive oil, plus more for greasing

4 teaspoons kosher salt

5 cups all-purpose flour, plus more for dusting

FOR SERVING

Softened butter

Extra-virgin olive oil

Balsamic vinegar

Flaky sea salt

The Italian bread basket is the hero of all restaurant appetizers. You know a place is good when you don't even have to order it—it just appears automatically. The best ones arrive still warm, wrapped in a napkin, served with little packets of soft butter. Olive oil and vinegar are close by, waiting for this moment. The bread itself is either a sliced loaf, dinner rolls, or breadsticks, all a little sweet, a little salty, and endlessly consumable. Lucky for me, my mom has a fantastic Italian bread recipe. She has spent decades baking endless loaves for every school fair, PTA event, church gathering, and Tupperware demonstration in Connecticut. But most importantly, she made it for us at home, and just like that restaurant bread basket, no one ordered it, but it was always there. With her permission, I'm revealing her secrets to the perfect Italian loaf, including how to transform it into the bread basket of your dreams.

1. Preheat the oven to 200°F, then turn it off when it reaches temperature.

2. In the biggest oven-safe bowl you own, combine the yeast with 2 cups of warm tap water and whisk until the yeast dissolves. Add the sugar, oil, and salt and whisk again until the sugar dissolves. Using a wooden spoon, stir in the flour until the dough forms into a shaggy ball. Lightly flour a clean work surface and turn out the dough. Knead the dough for 10 minutes until the dough forms a smooth ball. Alternatively, you can make the dough in a stand mixer fitted with the dough hook by mixing for about 5 minutes until the dough is smooth.

3. Clean out the large bowl, then lightly grease it with oil. Return the dough to the bowl and turn to coat with oil. Place a clean, damp kitchen towel over the bowl and transfer it to the warm oven. (Double check that the oven isn't on!) Let the dough rise there with the door closed for about 1 hour, until doubled in size. To test it, stick one finger into the dough. If the hole stays, my mom says you have done the job right.

Note

Wrap any extra loaves, rolls, or sticks tightly in cling wrap and store in the freezer for up to 6 months. To defrost, either leave on the counter overnight or heat at 400° for about 5 minutes, or until thawed.

4. Remove the bowl from the oven. Punch the dough down, cover it with the same towel, and let rise on the countertop until doubled in size again, about 1 hour more.

5. Preheat the oven to 400°F. Prepare the pan of your choosing (see below).

6. Lightly flour a clean work surface, turn out the dough, and punch it down again. Prepare the dough according to the instructions for your chosen format (see below again). Cover the pan(s) with damp kitchen towels and let rest at room temperature until the dough rises and fills out the pans, about 30 minutes.

7. Bake for 30 to 35 minutes, until the bread is nicely golden brown. Serve the bread hot, at room temperature, toasted, in a basket wrapped in a napkin—whatever your heart desires! Serve it with softened butter, olive oil, and balsamic vinegar for the authentic experience.

TO MAKE LOAVES: Use two 9 x 5-inch loaf pans. Divide the dough and place in the prepared loaf pans.

TO MAKE ROLLS: Use an 8 x 8-inch baking dish. Cut the dough into 9 equal pieces and roll them into tight balls. Arrange them in the prepared baking dish.

TO MAKE BREADSTICKS: Use a rimmed sheet pan lined with parchment paper. Roll the dough into an 8 x 10-inch rectangle, then cut it into eight 1-inch-wide strips. Arrange the strips on the prepared sheet pan.

Vegetables

GROSSY'S GUIDE TO ROASTING VEGETABLES

I'm a firm believer that every table needs at least one, but preferably multiple, veggies. Steamed, blanched, sautéed, fried—it doesn't matter as long as they're there! While you'll find so many ways to cook them, sometimes a busy mom like me needs to just throw them in the oven and focus on other things. On those days, I refer to this chart, a trusty guide to roasting vegetables, because I believe it's the easiest way to cook every vegetable.

First, wash and peel your vegetables. If there's cutting involved, be sure to cut into even-size pieces for even cooking. Then toss with olive oil (just enough to coat well), sprinkle with salt and pepper, and set on a rimmed sheet pan. Be sure to leave enough room for the vegetables to brown—if the pan is getting crowded, break out a second sheet pan. Vegetables that share an oven temp can bake together on separate sheet pans, as long as you remember to set two timers. If they share a temp *and* a time, go ahead and toss them all together! Most importantly, just like a Jersey girl down the shore, remember to flip halfway.

VEGETABLE	PREP	TEMP	TIME
Artichoke	Trimmed, wrapped in foil	400°F	90 minutes
Asparagus	Trimmed	400°F	15 minutes
Beet	Whole, wrapped in foil	400°F	60 minutes
Bell Pepper	Cut into strips	450°F	30 minutes
Broccoli	Cut into florets	400°F	30 minutes
Broccoli Rabe	Trimmed	425°F	15 minutes
Broccolini	Trimmed	425°F	15 minutes
Brussels Sprout	Trimmed and halved or quartered	450°F	30 minutes
Cabbage	Cored and cut into wedges	450°F	30 minutes
Carrot	Cut into 1-inch pieces	450°F	30 minutes
Cauliflower	Cut into florets	400°F	30 minutes
Celery Root	Cut into 1-inch pieces	425°F	20 minutes
Eggplant	Cut into 1-inch cubes	400°F	30 minutes
Endive	Trimmed and halved lengthwise	425°F	50 minutes
Fennel	Cored and cut into wedges	450°F	45 minutes
Green Bean	Trimmed	425°F	20 minutes
Leek	Cut into 1-inch pieces	400°F	30 minutes
Onion	Cut into wedges	400°F	30 minutes
Portobello Mushroom	Trimmed	450°F	15 minutes
Potato & Sweet Potato	Whole, wrapped in foil	350°F	60 minutes
	Cut into wedges	400°F	30 minutes
	Cut into 1-inch pieces	400°F	30 minutes
Radicchio	Cut into wedges	450°F	20 minutes
Radish	Halved or quartered	450°F	15 minutes
Squash			
ACORN	Cut into wedges	450°F	30 minutes
BUTTERNUT	Cut into 1-inch pieces	450°F	30 minutes
DELICATA	Sliced	450°F	30 minutes
SPAGHETTI	Halved and seeded	450°F	40 minutes
Zucchini	Sliced into rounds	450°F	15 minutes

Bimpy's Escarole & Beans

Serves 8

Kosher salt

2 large heads escarole, roughly chopped

2 tablespoons extra-virgin olive oil, plus more for serving

6 garlic cloves, crushed

1 tablespoon fennel seeds

½ teaspoon red pepper flakes

½ teaspoon freshly ground black pepper

3 (15-ounce) cans cannellini beans

4 cups chicken broth

Crusty bread and freshly grated Parmesan cheese, for serving

This dish is a pretty simple mix of ingredients—you probably already have everything at home, besides the escarole. All together, they turn into a warm and comforting mix of delicious flavors that feel like home, family, and troubles melting away. The smell and taste couldn't be more nostalgic for me. Somehow, whenever I go to Bimpy's house, he always has a pot of escarole and beans on the stove. Bimpy recommends serving over a nice chunk of crusty bread with Parmesan, a drizzle of olive oil, and a shout of "Say goodbye to your mother-in-law!" meaning it's so good it could kill someone with joy, and if it's going to kill someone, it should definitely be your mother-in-law. He has a singular sense of humor—what can I say? When I cook it at home, it makes me think of my dear uncle Phil, who lived with Bimpy until he passed away unexpectedly a few years ago. This dish was Phil's favorite, and when I miss him, which is often, I make this in his honor.

1. Bring a large Dutch oven filled with salted water to a boil. Add the escarole and cook until bright green and tender, 3 to 5 minutes. Reserve 2 cups of cooking water, then drain the escarole.

2. Wipe out the Dutch oven, then add the olive oil and heat it over medium-high heat. When the oil is shimmering, add the garlic, fennel seeds, pepper flakes, black pepper, and a pinch of salt. Cook, stirring frequently, until the garlic and fennel are fragrant, about 1 minute. Stir in the escarole and beans (including their liquid), then add the chicken broth. Give it a stir, then add as much reserved escarole water as you like (depending how soupy you want your dish).

3. Bring to a simmer and cook until the beans are warmed through, about 5 minutes. Taste for seasoning before serving with crusty bread and lots of Parmesan.

Creamy Cauliflower Skillet

Serves 4

1 (2-pound) head cauliflower

2 medium red onions

3 tablespoons extra-virgin olive oil

Kosher salt and freshly ground black pepper

4 garlic cloves, thinly sliced

8 ounces Fontina cheese, shredded

1 tablespoon fresh oregano leaves, roughly chopped

1 tablespoon fresh thyme leaves

1 cup heavy cream

½ cup white wine

Cauliflower is a true culinary hero. You can steam her, roast her, mash her, rice her, fry her, grill her. What can't she do? I honestly don't know. What I *do* know is that this recipe is one of her best looks ever. Large chunks are doused in a perfect mix of heavy cream, Fontina, and white wine, which creates the most-delicious-ever pool of sauce after roasting. The cauliflower gets tender and the onions caramelize perfectly. Topped with fresh herbs and served nice and warm, you will want to tuck yourself into this cozy skillet and never leave.

1. Preheat the oven to 450°F.

2. Trim the leaves and stem off the cauliflower, then cut the head into quarters. Arrange the pieces in a large cast-iron skillet. Trim the tops of the onions, but keep the roots intact. Remove the papery skin, then cut each onion into quarters. Arrange the pieces around the cauliflower.

3. Drizzle the olive oil over the veggies and rub to coat evenly. Season with salt and pepper. Scatter the garlic, Fontina, oregano, and thyme over the bottom of the skillet. Pour in the cream and white wine. Bake for 30 to 40 minutes, until the veggies are nicely browned and the cauliflower is knife-tender.

4. Serve this beauty straight from the skillet.

Four Seasons Salad

Serves 6

1 cup nuts or seeds

2 bunches lacinato kale, woody stems discarded and leaves sliced into ribbons

Juice of 1 lemon

2 tablespoons extra-virgin olive oil

Garlicky Citrus Dressing (page 37) or ¾ cup store-bought creamy vinaigrette

2 pounds roasted vegetables (see chart on page 97)

½ cup cheese, plus more for serving

Every girl needs her go-to salad. The whole point of salad, at least in my opinion, is to embrace the produce aisle, rotating ingredients in as they come into peak freshness with each season. After that, you want to balance texture and flavor to make every bite a delight. I especially love a farmers' market for inspiration, but I will be the first to admit that too many choices can be overwhelming. So I've made an easy guide (see below) to call out my favorite star veggie of each season, plus the crunchy and creamy elements that will go best with it. I encourage you to get creative and explore your own favorite combos as you get warmed up and inspired throughout the seasons. I find it helps to have a dressing that works with everything—luckily, my Garlicky Citrus Dressing is a total dream with produce all year round.

1. Place the nuts or seeds in a small skillet over medium heat. Cook, tossing occasionally, until toasted and fragrant, 3 to 5 minutes. Transfer to a small bowl.

2. Place the kale ribbons in a large bowl and add the lemon juice and olive oil. Use clean hands to coat and massage the kale. Add ¼ cup of the dressing and massage again. Let the kale rest for 5 minutes.

3. On a shallow platter (my preference) or in a big bowl, lay out the dressed kale—this is the foundation of your salad. Arrange the vegetables, cheese, and toasted nuts or seeds on top. Drizzle the remaining dressing all over and dig in.

SEASON	ROASTED VEGGIE	NUTS/SEEDS	CHEESE
WINTER	Cauliflower	Chopped walnuts	Blue cheese
SPRING	Asparagus	Sesame seeds	Burrata
SUMMER	Zucchini	Chopped almonds	Feta
FALL	Butternut squash	Pumpkin seeds	Freshly grated pecorino

Charred Garlicky Green Beans

Serves 4

3 tablespoons extra-virgin olive oil

12 ounces fresh green beans, trimmed

Kosher salt and freshly ground black pepper

Red pepper flakes

8 garlic cloves, thinly sliced

I have been cooking green beans like this for years, and every time I do, I think to myself, *How can something this simple be so delicious?* The answer lies in the aggressively hot skillet. Cooking food at super high temperatures can often feel like a mistake, but I promise you it's exactly what gives these beans lots of dark, delicious char and caramelizes the thinly sliced garlic. These beans are my idea of peak comfort food and the perfect quick side with anything.

1. Heat a large cast-iron or stainless steel skillet over medium heat until smoking hot, about 5 minutes. Add the olive oil and turn the skillet to coat the bottom evenly. Add the green beans and season with salt, black pepper, and pepper flakes. Use tongs to toss and stir the green beans until bright green and slightly softened, about 4 minutes.

2. Arrange the green beans in a single layer. Increase the heat to high and cook, undisturbed, until the green beans are charred and crisp-tender, 5 to 6 minutes. Add the garlic and cook, tossing to combine, until the garlic is fragrant and golden brown, 1 to 2 minutes.

3. Transfer the green beans and garlic to a platter, taste for seasoning, and serve.

Fresh Corn Polenta

Serves 4

1 teaspoon kosher salt, plus more as needed

1 cup dry polenta

4 tablespoons (½ stick) unsalted butter, cut into pieces

½ cup freshly grated Parmesan or pecorino cheese

2 ears of corn, kernels sliced from the cob, or 1½ cups frozen corn, thawed

In the '90s, my mom went through a serious polenta phase, creating every dish with it that you could possibly imagine. Soft, hard, fried, sweet, savory . . . honestly, it was a little unhinged. But somehow, even having survived that era, I *still* want to eat polenta all the time. It's a perfect base for so many meals, but I am here to tell you that almost nothing is better than a big bowl of warm polenta on its own. For the star treatment, I added the soft crunch of fresh corn kernels and the perfect balance of creamy butter and salty Parmesan. I wouldn't blame you if you add a dollop of mascarpone, or a jammy egg, or a little sausage, but I promise you this polenta stands up on her own!

1. Fill a medium saucepan with 3 cups of water and the salt. Bring to a boil over high heat. Slowly pour in the polenta, whisking constantly to avoid lumps. Cook according to the package directions.

2. Remove the saucepan from the heat. Stir in the butter, Parmesan, and corn kernels. Cover the saucepan and cook 3 to 4 minutes, until the butter is melted and the corn is warmed through. Stir again to distribute the melted butter. Taste for seasoning and serve.

Italian Baked Potato Bar

Serves 6

BAKED POTATOES

6 russet potatoes

¼ cup extra-virgin olive oil

Kosher salt and freshly ground black pepper

1 cup shredded mozzarella cheese

HERBY SOUR CREAM

1 (8-ounce) container sour cream

¼ cup finely chopped fresh herbs, such as basil, parsley, chives, rosemary, and/or thyme

Kosher salt

TOPPINGS

4 ounces cubed pancetta, cooked until crisp

Calabrian Chili Crisp (page 28) or store-bought chili crisp

Citrusy Olive Tapenade (page 29) or store-bought tapenade

Basil Almond Pesto (page 30) or store-bought pesto

BC Aioli (page 35) or store-bought aioli

Garlic Confit (page 36)

The idea of a buffet always gets my heart racing. As a kid, I loved an all-you-can-eat situation, the utensils and ingredients organized neatly, ready for you to dive in and create your own brand of madness. (Not surprisingly, that's exactly how I cook, too.) The buffet represents what I believe is a key part of entertaining: giving people options—and the baked potato is nothing if not a blank canvas for endless interpretations. Because the Italian in me can't help myself, we're going to quickly melt some mozz all over the split potato and set out a dreamy buffet of herby sour cream, crispy pancetta, and any number of Italiano condiments. All of this is optional and customizable—no matter what you choose, it will still be *molto buono.*

1. MAKE THE BAKED POTATOES: Preheat the oven to 350°F. Line a rimmed sheet pan with foil.

2. Wash and thoroughly dry the potatoes. Use the tines of a fork to poke the potato skins all over. Arrange the potatoes on the prepared sheet pan. Add the olive oil, salt, and pepper and toss to coat. Bake for about 1 hour, until knife-tender. Remove the sheet pan from the oven, but leave the oven on and keep the potatoes on the pan.

3. MEANWHILE, MAKE THE HERBY SOUR CREAM: In a medium bowl, combine the sour cream, herbs, and a pinch of salt. Stir to mix thoroughly. Cover tightly with cling wrap and refrigerate until ready to use.

4. Slice each potato lengthwise, taking care not to cut all the way through, and use tongs to pinch them open. Divide the mozzarella among the potatoes and return the sheet pan to the oven. Bake until the cheese is melted and starting to brown, 8 to 10 minutes.

5. Transfer the baked potatoes to a platter and arrange all the toppings around them, including the herby sour cream. Serve and let each person load up their own potato however they want!

Marinated Zucchini with Gremolata Vinaigrette

Serves 4 to 6

2 pounds zucchini

Kosher salt and freshly ground black pepper

½ cup Fresh Mint Gremolata (page 31)

¼ cup extra-virgin olive oil

¼ cup red wine vinegar

2 tablespoons roughly chopped roasted pistachios

You have never seen more zucchini in your life than in Bimpy's garden in the '80s. I know you think you have, but trust me on this. Bimpy and Grandma Katherine knew a million ways to make magic with their bumper crop, but their marinated zucchini remains a favorite. They soaked big pieces in oil and vinegar until the zucchini became saturated with flavor but still a little crisp. This dish is perfect on a hot summer day because it's cold, crunchy, and herby, especially with this cooling minty gremolata—plus, aren't we all always looking for ways to use up our zucchini by August? In this one, the flavors get better the longer the dish marinates, so by all means, make it ahead.

1. Slice the ends off the zucchini, then cut each zucchini lengthwise into quarters. Season heavily with salt and pepper. In a 9 x 13-inch baking dish or on a rimmed sheet pan, arrange the pieces, cut side down, in a single layer.

2. In a medium bowl, whisk together the gremolata, olive oil, vinegar, and a big pinch of salt. Spoon the marinade all over the zucchini. Wrap the baking dish tightly with cling wrap and refrigerate for at least 4 hours or preferably overnight.

3. Arrange the marinated zucchini on a platter and pour any accumulated juices over the top. Sprinkle on the chopped pistachios and serve.

Mom's Stuffed Artichokes

Serves 4

4 large globe artichokes

1½ cups panko breadcrumbs

1½ cups crushed Ritz Crackers (from 1 sleeve)

1 cup freshly grated Parmesan or pecorino cheese

2 large eggs, beaten

6 garlic cloves, grated

½ cup plus 1 tablespoon extra-virgin olive oil

1 teaspoon kosher salt

½ teaspoon freshly ground black pepper

1 lemon, sliced

AP Aioli or BC Aioli (page 35), for serving (optional)

The way an artichoke invites you to eat it—tearing it apart leaf by leaf with your hands, then claiming its meat by dragging each piece through your teeth—deserves its own investigation. It seems criminal, yet we do it unabashedly and with glee, especially in my family. Bimpy's mom made them, my mom made them, and her mom made them. Everyone's method was slightly different, and it's my mom's recipe that you'll find on my table most frequently. It's a total classic: The artichokes are stuffed with a mix of panko, Ritz Crackers, and tons of Parm, then steamed in a lemony bath. The result is soft, pillowy bites of heaven with a garlicky little crunch. I love aioli on the side for dipping, but these artichokes don't even need it!

1. Wash the artichokes thoroughly, then pat them dry with paper towels. Cut off the stems and carve a cross into the bottom of each artichoke. Slice about ¾ inch off the top of each artichoke, then spread the leaves apart.

2. In a medium bowl, stir together the panko, Ritz Crackers, Parmesan, eggs, garlic, olive oil, salt, and pepper. Holding one artichoke over the bowl, stuff about a quarter of the filling into each layer, working from the center out, until the leaves are fully separated. Place upright in a large Dutch oven. Repeat with the remaining artichokes and stuffing.

3. Pour about 1 inch of water into the bottom of the pot (take care not to get the stuffing wet) and tuck the lemon slices around the bottoms of the artichokes. Cover and set over high heat. As soon as the water comes to a boil, reduce the heat to low and simmer for about 45 minutes, adding more water to the pot as needed to keep the artichokes from drying out, until the artichokes are knife-tender.

4. Divide the artichokes among four plates and serve with aioli (if using) alongside for dipping, if you like.

Roasted Fennel, Orange & Olive Salad

Serves 4 to 6

½ cup red wine vinegar

½ cup extra-virgin olive oil

2 tablespoons spicy brown mustard

Kosher salt

Red pepper flakes

3 pounds fennel

1 small red onion, thinly sliced

2 large oranges, peel and pith trimmed, thickly sliced

½ cup oil-cured pitted black olives

½ cup Homemade Breadcrumbs (page 33) or store-bought panko breadcrumbs

Note
To make perfect orange slices, cut off the top and the bottom so you have two flat ends. Set the orange on one of the flat ends and run your knife from top to bottom, following its curve, to remove the peel and the bitter white pith—but ideally not too much fruit. Rotate the fruit as you slice away small sections. Once the flesh is showing, it's ready to be sliced.

During big family dinners, we always had a plate of fresh fennel on the table as a way to cleanse our palates between endless courses. Grandma Katherine was fennel's number one fan, and her favorite preparation by far was big chunks of it, sweet and caramelized from the oven. I think of her every time I make this salad, which pairs roasted fennel with citrus. Serve it warm or at room temperature with fresh slices of sweet orange, a smattering of black olives for briny saltiness, and fresh red onions for a tart crispness. Tossed in a perfectly simple vinaigrette, this salad is showy enough to be the center of your dinner, but understated enough to be a supporting player as well.

1. Preheat the oven to 450°F. Line a rimmed sheet pan with parchment paper.

2. In a large bowl, whisk together the vinegar, olive oil, mustard, and a pinch each of salt and pepper flakes. Taste for seasoning.

3. Cut the stems off the fennel, reserving some fronds for garnish. Keep the roots on and cut the bulbs into quarters. Add the fennel to the dressing and toss to coat. Arrange the fennel on the prepared sheet pan in a single layer. Roast for about 45 minutes, until the fennel is golden brown and knife-tender.

4. Remove the fennel from the oven and immediately transfer it back to the bowl with the dressing. Add the sliced onion and toss to coat. Set aside to marinate at room temperature for about 30 minutes.

5. Arrange the marinated fennel and the orange slices on a platter. Scatter the pickled red onions and the olives over the top. Whisk the remaining dressing in the bowl, then pour it over the salad. Finish with the breadcrumbs and a sprinkle of reserved fennel fronds. Serve.

Broccolini Panini

Serves 1

¼ cup hummus

½ teaspoon Calabrian chili paste or hot sauce, plus more as needed

2 tablespoons extra-virgin olive oil

1 bunch Broccolini, broccoli, or broccoli rabe, cut into 1-inch pieces

4 garlic cloves, thinly sliced

Kosher salt

Red pepper flakes

1 (4-inch) ciabatta loaf, halved lengthwise

4 slices provolone cheese

Note

If making multiple sandwiches that you need to keep warm for later, store them uncut and wrapped on a rimmed sheet pan in a 200°F oven.

Little Grossy was at his happiest at Bimpy's dinner table, stuffing garlicky Broccolini between hunks of bread and sprinkling it with grated Parmesan cheese. They were the perfect little sandwiches, even when sandwiches weren't on the menu. Big Grossy is at his happiest with leftover garlicky Broccolini in his fridge at all times—and I'm still making off-menu sandwiches, too. (For more on that, see page 146.) This perfect bite comes together in seconds, with a quick swipe of hummus for creaminess and Calabrian chili paste for a little heat. A small pile of broc and a little melty provolone get wrapped, pressed, and toasted all the way through.

1. In a small bowl, stir together the hummus and chili paste. Taste for spice level and add more chili paste as desired.

2. In a large skillet, heat the olive oil over medium heat. When the oil is shimmering, add the Broccolini and garlic, along with a big pinch each of salt and pepper flakes. Use tongs to turn and stir the Broccolini, cooking until very soft and wilted, about 8 minutes.

3. Meanwhile, lay out a piece of foil on a cutting board and lay an equal-size piece of parchment paper on top of the foil. Place the ciabatta on the parchment, cut sides up. Spread the spicy hummus on both halves, dividing evenly.

4. Use tongs to pile the Broccolini onto one half of the sandwich. (Don't forget those delicious garlic bits!) Lay 4 slices of provolone on top of the Broccolini, then gently press the other half of the bread on top to close her up. Wrap the sandwich tightly in the parchment paper, then wrap again in the foil.

5. Heat a grill pan or cast-iron skillet over medium heat. Place the wrapped sandwich on the grill pan, then place a Dutch oven or heavy skillet on top to press it down. Cook on one side for about 5 minutes, then flip the sandwich, press down, and cook for about 5 minutes more.

6. Return the sandwich to the cutting board and cut straight through the foil and parchment to halve the sandwich. Enjoy immediately if not sooner.

Whole-Roasted Eggplant with Calabrian Chili Crisp

Serves 2

1 medium globe eggplant (about 1 pound)

¼ cup Greek yogurt

¼ cup Calabrian Chili Crisp (page 28) or store-bought Calabrian chili paste, plus more for serving

I have to give credit to my dear friend Andy Baraghani for teaching me how to roast a whole eggplant. A lot of my life was spent slicing, dicing, roasting, and frying eggplant—and until Andy mentioned it, I'd never thought to just throw the whole thing in the oven and let it do its thing. The creamy, dreamy insides . . . I will honestly never recover from that first bite. To improve on the real-life fantasy, which doesn't even need improvement, a little Greek yogurt and Calabrian chili crisp enhance all the already-beautiful texture and flavor of the veg. A great payoff for very little work!

1. Preheat the oven to 350°F. Line a rimmed sheet pan with parchment paper.

2. Wash the eggplant, then pat the skin dry completely. Place the eggplant on the prepared sheet pan. Bake for 45 minutes to 1 hour, until the skin is wrinkly and the eggplant is extremely soft. Remove from the oven, cover with a clean kitchen towel, and let steam for 15 minutes. (This facial makes the insides extra soft and delicious.)

3. Meanwhile, in a small bowl, stir together the yogurt and chili crisp.

4. Transfer the whole eggplant to a serving platter (or don't). Slice it lengthwise, leaving the stem intact and taking care not cut all the way through. Use tongs to pry it open, then spoon the chili-yogurt mixture all over its flesh. Spoon a little more of the crisp over everything and serve.

Dough

What does it feel like to be the best mom ever? If you keep a batch of homemade pizza dough at the ready, you'll know soon enough!

Dough is one of the tentpoles of not only my cooking, but also my life. It's the foundation of all my bready dreams and perfect for getting creative in the kitchen. I especially love having it around when hosting, letting my guests get busy making their own customizable versions of pizza and calzones, or pulling warm rolls out of the oven to a round of applause.

I abide by one pizza dough recipe; it's simple to throw together and perfect for making ahead and refrigerating or freezing until it's time to bake. Best of all, it's versatile as all get-out.

What makes it so good? I thought you'd never ask.

WATER Beginning with warm water is the key to a perfect dough. Yeast responds best to water that's around 110°F, but no need to break out the thermometer to test. Just run the tap until the water is very comfortably *warm* without being at all hot. Being a little under temp is fine, but if the water is too hot, it will kill the yeast.

YEAST

Active dry yeast expires after a while, and that expiration date moves up if it's been exposed to too much heat or moisture. Storing your yeast in the refrigerator is a good way to keep it safe and even extend its life. But always be sure your yeast blooms after it's mixed with water—it will be slightly foamy and smell like bread—before adding anything else to the bowl.

SUGAR

Sugar doesn't sweeten the dough, but it does sweeten the deal with the yeast. Yeast is a bunch of living fungi, and their favorite food is sugar—so adding a little bit makes them extra active and gives your dough a super rise.

SALT

On the other hand, salt prohibits yeast growth. It goes in with the flour to help season the dough, after the yeast has had a head start on growing and expanding. Salt also helps build gluten structure, which is important for an airy, pliable dough.

FLOUR

Here we use bread flour, which has a higher protein content and therefore faster gluten development than, say, all-purpose. Gluten is the key to airy, chewy dough, and this recipe gets you there with minimal effort. Always be sure to measure your flour properly: Use a large spoon to scoop the flour into a measuring cup, then run a butter knife across the top to knock off the excess. Take care not to compact the flour as you're spooning or scraping!

KNEADING If you have a stand mixer, skip ahead (see note opposite). If not, don't fret! Cover your workspace with flour before turning out the dough and keep that flour nearby for extra coverage as needed. Use the heel of your hand to push down on the dough and stretch it out away from you. Fold the dough back over itself and rotate it slightly. Continue the process of stretch, fold, turn over and over until the dough is smooth and elastic. Continue adding flour as needed to help the process, but don't add too much or the dough will get dry and crumbly.

STORAGE This dough has a cold fermentation, which means the rising action happens in the fridge. All you need to do is grease the bowl (for easy release), cover it tightly (so all the gases can activate), and leave it alone (so it can get to work). The dough can ferment for up to 3 days in the refrigerator. The dough can also be frozen—after rising in the fridge overnight—and stored in the freezer for up to 6 months.

The Only Dough You'll Knead

Makes 2 pounds

1 tablespoon sugar

1 (¼-ounce) packet active dry yeast

1 tablespoon kosher salt

4 cups bread flour, plus more for dusting

Extra-virgin olive oil

The miracle of this chapter is that every recipe starts from this same pizza dough recipe.

Savory things are sweet, sweet things are savory, everything is warm and gooey for maximum yum. No matter what you fill it with, it's a welcome member at any and every party.

1. In a large bowl, combine the sugar, yeast, and 1¾ cups warm tap water. Let the mixture sit until foamy and fragrant, about 6 minutes.

2. Add the salt and flour. Use a wooden spoon to stir until a sticky dough forms.

3. Lightly flour a clean work surface and turn out the dough. Knead until it comes together into a soft, smooth, and slightly sticky dough, 3 to 5 minutes.

4. Drizzle a little bit of oil into the same large bowl, then return the dough to the bowl. Cover tightly with cling wrap and refrigerate overnight or up to 3 days.

5. To freeze the dough, if desired, divide it into two equal portions, roll them into balls, and wrap tightly with cling wrap. Set on a plate and freeze until solid, then transfer the frozen balls to a zip-top bag. Freeze for up to 6 months. Thaw the dough in the refrigerator overnight before using.

Note

You can also make this dough in a stand mixer using the dough hook attachment. After you mix all the ingredients together by hand, no need to turn the dough out—just knead it on high for about 5 minutes. Remove the bowl from the mixer, add some oil and rotate the dough to coat, then cover and refrigerate.

1. Garlic Parmesan Knots (page 138), 2. Festival Fried Dough (page 136),
3. Cheese Lover's Calzone (page 134), 4. Bimpy's Pizza (page 132),
5. Meaty Rolls (page 141), 6. Focaccia (page 137)

Bimpy's Pizza

Serves 6

2 pounds The Only Dough You'll Knead (page 123) or store-bought pizza dough

2 tablespoons olive oil

8 ounces grated mozzarella cheese

1¾ cups cups Blender Sauce (recipe opposite)

TOPPINGS

Freshly grated pecorino cheese

Fresh basil leaves

Red pepper flakes

Ah, the many variations of pizza. There's Neapolitan, Detroit-style, Chicago deep-dish, the classic Grandma slice . . . and then there's Bimpy's Pizza. Its thick crust, simple blender sauce, and layered cheese/sauce/cheese situation make it an instant classic. I had three separate conversations with Bimpy to get his recipe—he admitted he hadn't made it in a decade and was a little bit rusty. I was surprised to find out he bought the dough at a local pizzeria (honestly brilliant), blended but didn't cook the sauce (also brilliant), and basically didn't remember the rest (he's over one hundred, but he's still brilliant!). After playing around a bit, I can safely say I nailed it and now you can, too. The best part about this pizza is the flexibility. Obviously, I love my homemade dough, but live your store-bought fantasy if you want. The toppings can rotate (a pork sausage and broccoli rabe combo is a personal fave) and a drizzle of pesto (page 30) or a scoop of confit (page 36) is always welcome. This pizza is the right answer, no matter which way you slice it.

1. Preheat the oven to 500°F.

2. Spread the olive oil on a rimmed sheet pan, then use your hands to spread the pizza dough to the edges of the pan as much as possible. Place the sheet pan in a warm spot, like on top of the stove, and cover with a clean, damp kitchen towel. Let the dough rise for about 1 hour, until it easily spreads to cover the entire sheet pan.

3. Cover the dough with half of the mozzarella, leaving a ½-inch border all around. Spoon the sauce over the cheese, then sprinkle on the remaining mozzarella. Blanket the pizza with pecorino, a few basil leaves, a pinch of pepper flakes, and/or whatever other toppings ring your bell. Truly, the options are limitless—have fun with it!

4. Bake the pizza for 20 to 30 minutes, until the crust is golden brown and the cheese is bubbling. Slice and serve directly from the pan with extra pecorino and pepper flakes.

Blender Sauce

Makes about 3½ cups

1 (28-ounce) can tomato puree
or crushed tomatoes

4 garlic cloves

¼ cup fresh basil leaves

4 anchovy fillets

In a blender or food processor, combine the tomatoes, garlic, basil, and anchovies. Listen closely: The anchovies are not optional. Blend on high until smooth, about 1 minute. Transfer to an airtight container and store refrigerated for up to 1 week.

Calzones

Calzones were a pizza shop favorite of my childhood, like a beautiful purse filled with the promise of steamy, ooey-gooey fabulousness. Like pizzas, calzones offer endless options, and I love hosting a make-your-own calzone party, giving my friends fun filling choices. Cheese, meats, veggies, marinara inside or outside for dipping or both . . . you can't possibly take a wrong turn. These are two of my favorite combos, but by all means go off and find your own path to greatness.

Cheese Lover's

Makes 4 calzones

15 ounces whole-milk ricotta

8 ounces Fontina cheese, grated

8 ounces shredded mozzarella cheese

4 ounces goat cheese

½ cup freshly grated Parmesan or pecorino cheese

1 tablespoon finely chopped fresh basil leaves

1 tablespoon fresh thyme leaves

1 teaspoon dried oregano

½ teaspoon kosher salt

½ teaspoon freshly ground black pepper

½ teaspoon red pepper flakes

2 pounds The Only Dough You'll Knead (page 123) or store-bought pizza dough

All-purpose flour, for dusting

2 large eggs, beaten

Grossy's Marinara (page 153) or store-bought marinara, for serving

1. Preheat the oven to 400°F with the racks set in the upper and lower thirds. Line two rimmed sheet pans with parchment paper.

2. In a large bowl, combine the ricotta, Fontina, mozzarella, goat cheese, Parmesan, basil, thyme, oregano, salt, black pepper, and pepper flakes. Stir to mix well.

3. Divide the pizza dough into 4 equal pieces. Lightly flour a clean work surface, then roll out one of the dough pieces into a roughly 8-inch oval. Brush the border of the oval with some of the beaten egg.

4. Scoop a quarter of the cheese mixture (1 heaping cup) into the center of the oval and spread it out until just shy of the egg-washed border. Fold the dough over itself longways so the eggy edges are touching and the ingredients are enclosed. Dip a fork into flour and press all around the edges of the calzone to seal firmly. Transfer the calzone to a prepared sheet pan and brush the top with more egg wash. Repeat with the remaining dough, egg wash, and filling, arranging two calzones on each sheet pan.

5. Bake for about 30 minutes, swapping the sheet pans halfway, until the dough is deep golden brown. Serve the calzones with marinara alongside for dipping.

Meat Lover's

Makes 4 calzones

½ pound Italian sausage, casings removed

1 large white onion, diced

1 green bell pepper, diced

Kosher salt and freshly ground black pepper

4 ounces cubed ham

½ cup pepperoni slices, halved

2 pounds The Only Dough You'll Knead (page 123) or store-bought pizza dough

All-purpose flour for dusting

2 large eggs, beaten

1 cup whole-milk ricotta

1 cup Blender Sauce (page 133), Grossy's Marinara (page 153), or store-bought marinara sauce, for serving

1. Preheat the oven to 400°F with the racks set in the upper and lower thirds. Line two rimmed sheet pans with parchment paper.

2. In a medium nonstick skillet, cook the sausage over medium heat, using a wooden spoon to break up the meat, until no longer pink, about 5 minutes. Use a slotted spoon to transfer the sausage to a large bowl, reserving the fat in the skillet.

3. To the skillet, add the onion, green pepper, and a large pinch each of salt and pepper. Cook, stirring occasionally, until the veggies are just beginning to soften, about 5 minutes. Transfer the veggies to the bowl with the sausage. Add the ham and pepperoni and stir to combine everything.

4. Divide the pizza dough into 4 equal pieces. Lightly flour a clean work surface, then roll out one of the dough pieces into a roughly 8-inch oval. Brush the border of the oval with some of the beaten egg.

5. Dollop ¼ cup of the ricotta into the center of the oval and spread it out until just shy of the egg-washed border. Scoop a quarter of the meat mixture (1 packed cup) into the center of the oval and spread it over the ricotta. Fold the dough over itself so the eggy edges are touching and the ingredients are enclosed. Dip a fork into flour and press all around the edges of the calzone to seal firmly. Transfer the calzone to a prepared sheet pan and brush the top with more egg wash. Repeat with the remaining dough, filling, and egg wash, arranging two calzones on each sheet pan.

6. Bake for about 30 minutes, swapping the sheet pans halfway, until the dough is deep golden brown. Serve immediately with Blender Sauce alongside for dipping.

Festival Fried Dough

Serves 8

2 quarts vegetable oil, for frying

2 pounds The Only Dough You'll Knead (page 123) or store-bought pizza dough

Toppings of choice (see below)

Italian heritage festivals, church carnivals, county fairs—if dough was being fried for any of these occasions within a three-state radius, I made my parents pack up the car and take me! One of my favorite places to get my fix was Blink's Fry Doe in Hampton Beach, New Hampshire. We went there every summer for vacation, and while everyone else was excited about the beach, I couldn't wait to get to the boardwalk and head to Blink's. Their fried dough was at least a foot long, and they offered an endless list of toppings, which I would read through every time I went, which was daily, just to make sure a new one hadn't been added. (I have provided a similar list of toppings for you here, but please let me know when you add a new one—I can't not know.) Even a simple dusting of powdered sugar is the perfect accompaniment to the greasy, crunchy, fluffy, piping-hot rectangle of delicious fried dough.

1. Clip a deep-fry thermometer to the side of a large Dutch oven and set it over medium heat. Add the vegetable oil and heat it to 400°F.

2. Meanwhile, divide the pizza dough into 8 equal pieces. Stretch one of the dough pieces into a roughly 6-inch circle. Carefully lower the dough into the oil. Cook until golden brown on both sides, 4 to 6 minutes total, using tongs to flip the dough halfway through. Transfer the dough to paper towels to drain. Continue frying the dough, allowing the oil to return to 400°F before stretching and frying each piece.

3. Top the fried dough with your fantasy combo and serve, preferably on paper plates, while still hot.

Classic Toppings

Applesauce & Cinnamon Sugar

Blueberry Pie Filling

Cinnamon Sugar

Honey & Chopped Walnuts

Marinara & Parmesan

Melted Butter & Garlic

Nutella & Powdered Sugar

Peanut Butter & Jelly (a Grossy favorite)

Powdered Sugar

Shredded Coconut

Whipped Cream & Sprinkles

Focaccia

Makes One 9 x 13-inch focaccia

Extra-virgin olive oil, for greasing

2 pounds The Only Dough You'll Knead (page 123) or store-bought pizza dough

Toppings of choice (see below)

I'll admit, focaccia and I did not fall in love at first sight. Many times throughout my youth, a basket of focaccia was placed in front of me, and I sat there unmoved. I hardly ever pass up anything that looks remotely like bread and is served in a basket, so this nonreaction was notable. Not until I studied abroad in Rome did it finally click for me: you can have focaccia with any meal, with any topping, with any filling. It can be thick, it can be thin. And, most importantly, it can be sweet or savory. When I realized all its many ways, shapes, and forms, I came around. As a surprise to no one, I favor an extra-thick focaccia, so I make mine in a baking dish, which yields a soft inside and a perfectly crunchy outside. From there, it's a canvas, and I'm the artist.

1. Generously coat a 9 x 13-inch baking dish or rimmed sheet pan with olive oil. Place the dough in the baking dish and use clean hands to gently spread it as far as it will stretch. Cover with a clean kitchen towel and set aside until the dough has slightly risen and is easily pliable, about 1 hour.

2. Preheat the oven to 450°F.

3. Uncover the dough and continue to press it until it reaches the edges of the pan, leaving lots of finger indents all over. Add before-baking toppings, if desired.

4. Bake for 20 to 30 minutes until the top is deep golden brown. Remove from the oven and let cool for at least 30 minutes before adding any after-baking toppings, slicing, and serving.

Sweet Toppings

BEFORE BAKING

Halved figs

Halved seedless grapes

Sliced peaches

Sliced plums

Sliced strawberries

Sugar (granulated, brown, or a mix)

Thinly sliced apples

AFTER BAKING

Balsamic Drizzle (page 29) or store-bought balsamic glaze

Cinnamon sugar

Nutella

Orange zest

Powdered sugar

Savory Toppings

BEFORE BAKING

Artichoke hearts

Capers

Flaky sea salt

Garlic Confit (page 36)

Pitted olives

Shredded cheese

Thinly sliced cured meat

Tomato Confit (page 36)

AFTER BAKING

Basil Almond Pesto (page 30) or store-bought pesto

Calabrian Chili Crisp (page 28) or store-bought chili crisp

Citrusy Olive Tapenade (page 29) or store-bought tapenade

Fresh herbs

Knots

I have to thank my longtime roommates, Tyler and Dakota, for bringing knots back into my adult life after a childhood full of them. The way that these two embrace the menu at our local pizza joint (shout-out to Rocco Pizza III in Bed-Stuy!) makes me smile like the proudest mom. Adventurous pizza toppings, mozzarella sticks, buffalo wings . . . and, yes, both garlic *and* sweet knots. They order them; I eat them. It's just understood. Always up for some fun in the kitchen, the boys and I started playing around with making our own knots, and things got too good knot to share. These easy twists have a hidden surprise inside (gooey mozz in the garlic knots; melted chocolate in the cinnamon knots) that make them insanely delicious and impossible to walk away from.

Garlic Parmesan Knots

Makes 16 knots

All-purpose flour, for dusting

2 pounds The Only Dough You'll Knead (page 123) or store-bought pizza dough

32 mozzarella pearls from 1 (8-ounce) container

1 cup (2 sticks) unsalted butter, melted

4 garlic cloves, minced

3 tablespoons freshly grated Parmesan or pecorino cheese

1 tablespoon minced fresh parsley

1. Preheat the oven to 400°F. Line two rimmed sheet pans with parchment paper.

2. Lightly flour a clean work surface, then roll out the dough into a 10 x 16-inch rectangle. Use a pizza cutter or sharp knife to slice 16 (1-inch-wide) strips. Loop the two ends through each other to tie each strip of dough into a knot and nestle 2 mozzarella pearls into the center of each. Arrange 8 knots on each prepared sheet pan, spacing them 2 inches apart. Brush the knots with half of the melted butter. Bake for 25 to 30 minutes, until nicely golden brown.

3. Meanwhile, in a small bowl, stir together the garlic, Parmesan, and parsley. Remove the knots from the oven, brush them with the remaining butter, and sprinkle the garlic mixture generously over the tops. Serve hot.

Cinnamon Sugar Knots

Makes 16 knots

All-purpose flour, for dusting

2 pounds The Only Dough You'll Knead (page 123) or store-bought pizza dough

32 milk chocolate squares from 3 (1.55-ounce bars)

½ cup (1 stick) unsalted butter, melted

1 tablespoon ground cinnamon

1 tablespoon sugar

1. Preheat the oven to 400°F. Line two rimmed sheet pans with parchment paper.

2. Lightly flour a clean work surface, then roll out the dough into a 10 x 16-inch rectangle. Use a pizza cutter or sharp knife to slice 16 (1-inch-wide) strips. Loop the two ends through each other to tie each strip of dough into a knot and nestle two chocolate squares into the center of each. Arrange 8 knots on each prepared sheet pan, spacing them 2 inches apart. Brush the knots with half of the melted butter. Bake for 25 to 30 minutes, until nicely golden brown.

3. Meanwhile, in a small bowl, stir together the cinnamon and sugar. Remove the knots from the oven, brush them with the remaining butter, and sprinkle the cinnamon sugar generously over the tops. Serve hot.

Rolls

Baking a batch of cinnamon rolls is how I wake up the house on Christmas morning, New Year's Day, Easter Sunday, and every vacation day in every vacation house I have ever rented. All this is to say: they are very important to me. After much experimenting over the years, I've found that pizza dough is a great way to make the soft, thick, gooey cinnamon roll I'm always craving. Smother them with cream cheese frosting and *boom*, you can have Christmas in July in your Airbnb. Different, but of equal importance in my life, is stromboli, a savory stuffed bread that is rolled, baked, sliced, and served warm. The swirls of stromboli aren't that far from cinnamon rolls, except the pizza dough is stuffed with mozzarella, provolone, and the Italian cured meats of your dreams.

Sweetie

Makes 9 rolls

Butter, for greasing

All-purpose flour, for dusting

2 pounds The Only Dough You'll Knead (page 123) or store-bought pizza dough

1½ cups packed light brown sugar

3 tablespoons ground cinnamon

½ cup (1 stick) unsalted butter, melted

2 (8-ounce) packages cream cheese, at room temperature

1 cup powdered sugar

1 teaspoon pure vanilla extract

¼ teaspoon kosher salt

1. Grease the bottom and sides of a 9 x 13-inch baking dish.

2. Lightly flour a clean work surface and turn out the dough. Flour the top of the dough, then roll it into a 14 x 10-inch rectangle, with one of the longer sides closest to you. (If the dough is resistant, cover it with a clean kitchen towel and let it rest for about 10 minutes until pliable.)

3. In a medium bowl, whisk together the brown sugar and cinnamon. Brush half of the melted butter over the surface of the dough, then sprinkle the sugar mixture over the top. Drizzle the remaining melted butter over the sugar mixture.

4. Beginning with the long edge closest to you, roll the dough into a tight log, pressing lightly to be sure the dough doesn't catch any air pockets. Slice the log into nine 1½-inch-thick rolls. Nestle the rolls into the prepared baking dish in three rows of three, one in the center and two at either end of the baking dish, leaving about 2 inches between each row. Cover the baking dish with a clean kitchen towel and let rest for about 30 minutes, until the dough rises slightly.

5. Preheat the oven to 350°F.

6. Uncover the baking dish and bake the rolls for 30 to 40 minutes, until they have filled out the baking dish and the sugar filling is bubbling. Remove the rolls from the oven and let them cool in the baking dish for about 30 minutes.

7. Meanwhile, in a medium bowl, whisk together the cream cheese, powdered sugar, vanilla, and salt. After the rolls have cooled, use a spoon to scoop and swirl the frosting over them. Serve immediately, or a little bit later when everyone wakes up.

Meaty

Makes 9 rolls

All-purpose flour, for dusting

The Only Dough You'll Knead (page 123) or store-bought pizza dough

¼ cup extra-virgin olive oil, plus more for greasing

2 tablespoons minced garlic

8 ounces thinly sliced provolone cheese

8 ounces thinly sliced mozzarella cheese

3 ounces sliced Genoa salami

3 ounces sliced sandwich-style pepperoni

3 ounces sliced capicola or coppa

Freshly grated Parmesan or pecorino cheese and dried parsley, for topping

1. Grease the bottom and sides of a 9 x 13-inch baking dish.

2. Lightly flour a clean work surface and turn out the dough. Flour the top of the dough, then roll it into a 14 x 10-inch rectangle, with one of the longer sides closest to you. (If the dough is resistant, cover it with a clean kitchen towel and let it rest for about 10 minutes until pliable.)

3. Brush the surface of the dough with olive oil and sprinkle the garlic over the top. Arrange the provolone and mozzarella all over the dough. Stack the salami on a cutting board and cut the slices into quarters, then sprinkle the pieces over the cheese. Do the same with pepperoni and capicola slices.

4. Beginning with the long edge closest to you, roll the dough into a tight log, pressing lightly to be sure the dough doesn't catch any air pockets. Slice the log into nine 1½-inch-thick rolls. Nestle the rolls into the prepared baking dish in three rows of three, one in the center and two at either end of the baking dish, leaving about 2 inches between each row. Cover the baking dish with a clean kitchen towel and let rest for about 30 minutes, until the dough rises slightly.

5. Preheat the oven to 350°F.

6. Uncover the baking dish and bake the rolls for 30 to 40 minutes, until they have filled out the baking dish and the cheese is golden brown. Remove the rolls from the oven and let them cool in the baking dish for about 30 minutes.

7. Top the rolls with plenty of Parmesan and dried parsley. Let cool completely or serve immediately.

The Big Italian Sandwich

GROSSY'S GUIDE TO THE PERFECT SANDWICH

My heart (and stomach, but same thing) is always on the lookout for the *perfect* sandwich. Nothing brings me greater joy than that one gorgeous bite in which every ingredient is perfectly aligned and combined. While I do have an ultimate Barbie Dream~~house~~ Italian sandwich, and I'll tell you all about it, I want to chat about the *why* before we get into the *how*.

BREAD

Arguably the most important part of any sandwich, the bread has to be good. It should have some crunch but still be soft enough that your gums and the roof of your mouth don't feel threatened. It should squish when you bite into it but not flatten out completely. It should be everything all at once, and I don't think that's too much to ask.

MEATS

Prepacked is totally fine; freshly sliced at the counter even better; leftovers from a roast the night before, the best. Either way, the meat has to be draped and folded onto the sandwich to give it texture and volume. That's what makes each bite interesting!

CHEESE

Lay it flat in a beautiful shelf, leaving no gaps. We don't skimp on cheese here.

CONDIMENTS

Sandwich time is *not* the time to be polite. Mayo, oil and vin, mustard, dressing—whatever it is, there needs to be a lot of it. Nothing is more upsetting than a sad, dry sandwich.

VEGGIES

Tomatoes, onions, peppers, olives, pickles—take your pick, mix and match, but whatever you do, make sure they're thinly sliced. They're here to support, not take over. The only exception is a vegetarian sub, which should obviously consist of thick bites of veggies.

LETTUCE

Similarly, whatever your choice of lettuce type and shape (I flip between iceberg and romaine) it needs to be in unreasonable quantities. Half of it will end up falling out and that is the whole point. I like to cut my lettuce into thin shreds and pile it on by the fistful.

THE ORDER OF OPERATIONS

Start with the bread and smother both sides in condiments. Then pile on the meats, working from the heaviest to lightest cuts so the layers stay pillowy. ➡

Cheese comes next, followed by any veggies. Drizzle on more condiments as needed, then gently press the top on.

Secret Sandwiches

When I was six years old, my dad and Bimpy took me to Yankee Stadium. It wasn't until we were settled into our seats that Bimpy revealed he had smuggled in a few sandwiches. Before we left for the game that morning, he scooped leftover eggplant parm onto bread, wrapped the rolls up tight, and hid them somewhere (we're still not sure where, and he still won't tell us). So the fact that I view most leftovers as future sandwiches is a genetic trait. In the tradition of Bimpy, here is a list of all the secret sandwiches throughout this book. I promise this is the most delicious scavenger hunt you've ever been on.

Dad's Egg Salad *(page 46)*
Ready to be spooned between two slices of sandwich bread with a pile of iceberg and a tomato slice.

Marinated Zucchini with Gremolata Vinaigrette *(page 111)*
Toast slices of crusty bread covered with cheese slices, then pile the zucchini on.

Gigantic Meatballs *(page 162)*
Toast slices of focaccia blanketed with cheese, then cut the meatballs in half and line them up on the sandwich. For bonus points, top the meatballs with fried eggs and hot sauce.

Beany Zucchini Balls *(page 164)*, **Eggplant Parmesan** *(page 166)*, **and Prosciutto & Mozzarella–Stuffed Chicken Parm** *(page 168)*
These are all begging to be in a hoagie roll with extra marinara and cheese.

Porchetta *(page 221)*
Nestle it between sliced ciabatta halves with heavily dressed greens and a roasted red pepper or two.

Sausage & Peppers & Potatoes & Onions *(page 226)*
All that's missing is the hoagie roll and cheese!

Live, Loaf, Love *(page 229)*
Two slices of soft bread, a heavy slather of mayo, and you're one bite away from heaven.

Tagliata di Manzo *(page 237)*
All the elements for a perfect steak sandwich on a toasted baguette.

The Big Italian Sandwich

Serves 1 to 6

VEGGIE AIOLI

½ cup chopped Giardiniera (page 32) or store-bought giardiniera

½ cup chopped pitted Castelvetrano olives

½ cup BC or AP Aioli (page 35) or store-bought mayonnaise

2 tablespoons red wine vinegar

2 teaspoons dried oregano

1 teaspoon freshly ground black pepper

Kosher salt

SANDWICH

2 beefsteak tomatoes, thinly sliced

Kosher salt and freshly ground black pepper

1 large (12 to 14-inch) loaf Italian bread

6 ounces sliced Genoa salami

6 ounces sliced sandwich-style pepperoni

6 ounces sliced capicola or coppa

6 ounces sliced prosciutto

4 ounces sliced provolone

1 cup sliced banana peppers (from a 17-ounce jar)

½ cup sliced black olives (from a 7-ounce can)

4 cups shredded iceberg lettuce

If a deli has an Italian sandwich on their menu, I'm ordering it—no question. And if they don't, I am still ordering it, because I know exactly how I want it, and I am not afraid to say so. This sandwich is not for the faint of heart or polite eaters. While great joy can be derived from ordering an Italian deli sandwich, perhaps an even greater joy can be found in re-creating that deli energy in your own home. This sandwich is big—REALLY big—piled high with the best cured meats, Italian cheeses, fresh veggies, and condiments that make my (and hopefully your) dreams come true, every time.

1. MAKE THE VEGGIE AIOLI: In a medium bowl, combine the giardiniera, olives, aioli, vinegar, oregano, pepper, and a big pinch of salt. Stir together well and taste for seasoning.

2. MAKE THE SANDWICH: Arrange the tomato slices on a large plate and season generously with salt and pepper.

3. Use a serrated knife to halve the loaf lengthwise and lay the halves cut sides up on a cutting board. Spread the veggie aioli over both halves of the bread. It might seem a little runny at first, but the bread will absorb the aioli, creating a delicious canvas for your sandwich.

4. Fold the salami, pepperoni, capicola, and prosciutto and drape the meat over the bottom half of the sandwich. Layer the provolone over the meat. Arrange the tomato slices over the cheese, then pile on the banana peppers and olives. Pack on the ribbons of lettuce, then press the top of the sandwich down.

5. Use the serrated knife to cut down the center of the sandwich and serve.

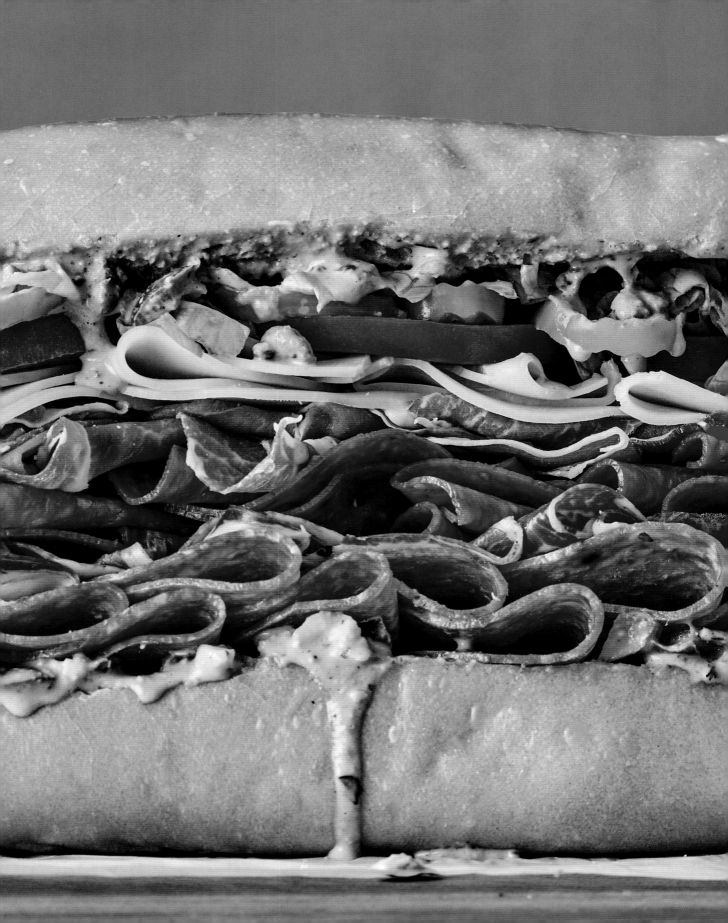

Marinara

Nothing is more central to the Italian American diet than Italian gravy, Sunday sauce, a pot of maranad. (Also complaining about the agita [Italian heartburn] after your third plate.)

Bimpy and Grandma Katherine always had a pot of marinara on the stove, another pot in the fridge, and many containers in the multiple freezers around the basement. In the summer, their garden exploded with neon-red tomatoes and gigantic basil leaves. Throughout the rest of the year, their shelves were stacked high with canned tomatoes. When I moved to California in my twenties, the only way I knew how to deal with the creeping homesick feeling was to make marinara. So I would pull out my biggest pot, call in advice from every family member who had ever touched a tomato, and start filling my tiny apartment with batch after batch until it smelled like home.

A simmering pot of marinara is one of the simplest pleasures in life, but you have to put care into each component to achieve nonna-level sauce.

 **TOMATO**

I use three types of tomatoes in my marinara: fresh, pureed, and paste. The fresh add a perfect texture: choose plum tomatoes that are red, ripe, and still firm. The cans of puree add body: stick to your favorite brand and avoid added seasoning or reduced salt. And the paste adds extra-rich flavor: again, pick your favorite—we want a classic can or tube of the good stuff for the best results.

WINE

If you wouldn't sip a glass of it, it doesn't belong here. But price doesn't always equal quality—all you need for a marinara is a nice, dry red with lots of character. As the wine cooks down, all the natural flavors concentrate to make the base of a sauce that's complex and perfectly layered.

SUGAR

A controversial marinara ingredient, sugar is either the banned-for-life or must-have ingredient in red sauce. I think a spoonful or two helps wake up all the flavors, round out the marinara, and enhance the sweet tomato flavor. But if you can feel your ancestors rolling in their graves, leave it out.

ALLIUMS

I use red onion for maximum flavor, and an even dice helps it soften perfectly into the final sauce. On the other hand, I go for a rough chop with my garlic because I love a surprise bite here and there. If you want it to blend in, mincing or using a garlic press is totally fine.

SEASONINGS

Even dried spices eventually expire, so be sure your dried oregano is still packing a punch and your red pepper flakes are still fiery hot. Freshly ground peppercorns release a lot of flavor that the pre-ground stuff just doesn't. And choose basil that is vibrant and fragrant. Most importantly, taste often and season well.

GARLIC BREAD

I wouldn't dream of serving anything marinara related without a generous helping of garlic bread. This quick and easy recipe serves 6 to 8 people and basically throws itself together in no time. Set your broiler on high. Slice a baguette in half lengthwise and place it cut side up on a sheet pan lined with foil. In a small bowl, stir together 4 tablespoons softened unsalted butter, 4 grated garlic cloves, ¼ teaspoon kosher salt, ¼ teaspoon freshly ground black pepper, ¼ teaspoon red pepper flakes, and ¼ teaspoon smoked paprika. Spread the butter mixture onto both halves of the baguette. Broil for 2 to 4 minutes, until the bread is golden brown and toasted. Cut the bread into slices and garnish with chopped parsley.

Grossy's Marinara

Makes 8 cups

2 tablespoons extra-virgin olive oil

1 medium red onion, diced

10 garlic cloves, roughly chopped

Kosher salt and freshly ground black pepper

Red pepper flakes

1 cup red wine

2 tablespoons dried oregano

2 pounds medium plum tomatoes, quartered

2 (28-ounce) cans tomato puree

1 (6-ounce) can tomato paste

A handful fresh basil leaves, roughly torn

Sugar, as needed

No two cooks make marinara the same way, and no two pots are ever exactly the same, but that's the beauty of the sauce. This method is my tried-and-true, developed over decades of trial and error, but the door is wide open for interpretation. Use what you love and be open to tweaking it as you aim for your idea of perfection. The only goal is a simmering sauce that you want to slather over everything—and slather it you will, in all the recipes in this chapter.

1. In a large Dutch oven, heat the olive oil over medium heat. When the oil is shimmering, add the onion, garlic, and a generous pinch each of salt, black pepper, and red pepper flakes. Cook, stirring occasionally, until the onion is soft and the garlic is beginning to brown, about 6 minutes. Add the wine and oregano and simmer until the wine is reduced by about half, 6 to 8 minutes.

2. Add the quartered tomatoes and cover the pot. Cook, covered but stirring and smashing the tomatoes occasionally with a wooden spoon, until the tomatoes are mostly broken down, about 20 minutes. Add the tomato puree, tomato paste, basil, and another pinch of salt. Reduce the heat to low and simmer, stirring occasionally, until the flavors develop and the sauce thickens. This can go on for hours, but about 20 minutes is the minimum.

3. Taste for seasoning, adding more salt, black pepper, red pepper flakes, and the sugar, as needed. Serve immediately or let cool completely in the pot. Store refrigerated in the pot for up to 3 days and reheat over low heat before serving, or transfer the cooled sauce to freezer-safe containers and store frozen for up to 6 months, thawing in the refrigerator a day before using.

Gigantic Meatballs

Makes 8 gigantic meatballs

1½ pounds ground beef (85% lean because we need that fat)

1½ pounds ground pork

1½ cups Homemade Breadcrumbs (page 33) or store-bought panko breadcrumbs

Large handful chopped fresh basil leaves

Large handful chopped fresh mint leaves

1 cup freshly grated Parmesan cheese, plus more for serving

1 cup raisins

3 large eggs

1 teaspoon kosher salt

1 teaspoon freshly ground black pepper

1 teaspoon red pepper flakes

8 cups Grossy's Marinara (page 153) or store-bought marinara sauce

2 tablespoons extra-virgin olive oil

Cooked pasta of your choice, such as spaghetti, for serving

Garlic bread (see page 152), for serving (optional)

On any given day when I call up Bimpy and ask him what he's doing, he will most likely reply, "Making meatballs?" in a tone that questions the audacity of my question. Bimpy's meatballs were the gigantic centerpiece (literally, these are the biggest meatballs you've ever seen) of every single meal our family ate at his house, and I learned a lot from watching him construct them. As I began cooking my own meatballs in my early twenties, I kept a lot of what he taught me, like the raisins, which are an old Sicilian tradition, and added a few elements of my own, like fresh mint and homemade breadcrumbs. And that's how basically all my recipes come to be: respect for the past with a dash of the present, which is the best way to cook. After we crisp up the outsides, the meatballs simmer in the marinara to cook through while staying moist. The flavors meld, taking the dish to a place you have never thought possible.

1. In a large bowl, combine the beef and pork, breaking up the meat as you add it. Add the breadcrumbs, basil, mint, Parmesan, raisins, eggs, salt, black pepper, and pepper flakes and use your hands to mix until all the ingredients are evenly distributed. Divide the mixture evenly and round it into 8 firmly packed meatballs, each about the size of a baseball. (I told you, these are gigantic!)

2. In a large pot, heat the marinara, covered, over low heat.

3. Meanwhile, in a large skillet, heat the oil over medium heat. When the oil is shimmering, add half the meatballs. Cook, turning occasionally, until crispy and dark on the outside, about 10 minutes total. Immediately transfer the meatballs to the pot of marinara. Submerge them in the sauce, re-cover the pot, and continue simmering. Repeat with the remaining meatballs.

4. Remove the skillet from the heat and add a few ladles of marinara to it. Use a wooden spoon to scrape up the browned bits from the bottom, then pour the marinara back into the pot with the meatballs.

5. Again, check that your meatball children are fully submerged, then replace the lid, tell them you love them, and wish them luck. Simmer for about 20 minutes; the only way to know if your meatballs are fully cooked is to discreetly cut into one to see its center. If it's just barely pink, you are there.

6. Spoon both the meatballs and marinara over a bowl of pasta and sprinkle with more Parmesan. Serve with a plate of garlic bread for ultimate joy, if you like.

Note
Bimpy literally makes one hundred meatballs regularly just to freeze. If you want to be like Bimpy, do so *before* you drop the meatballs into the sauce. After searing, let cool completely, then place them in a zip-top bag and freeze. When you are ready to use them, defrost overnight in the refrigerator, then proceed with the marinara simmer to finish cooking and warm through.

Beany Zucchini Balls

Serves 4

3 pounds zucchini, grated

2 tablespoons kosher salt

1 (15.5-ounce) can cannellini beans, drained and rinsed

2 large eggs

3 cups Homemade Breadcrumbs (page 33) or store-bought panko breadcrumbs

1 cup raisins

½ cup pine nuts (optional)

½ cup freshly grated Parmesan or pecorino cheese

2 tablespoons chopped fresh basil

2 tablespoons chopped fresh mint

1 teaspoon freshly ground black pepper

1 teaspoon red pepper flakes

1 (8-ounce) container mozzarella pearls, drained

1 cup extra-virgin olive oil

2 cups Grossy's Marinara (page 153) or store-bought marinara sauce

Garlic bread (see page 152), for serving (optional)

Beans, beans, they're good for your heart, the more you eat, the more you . . . well, you know the rest. As a self-proclaimed Meatball making meatballs, I can confidently say that not all meatballs contain meat. While these contain similar notes to my Gigantic Meatballs (raisins, basil, mint; see more on page 162), they are very much their own moment. A mix of shredded zucchini and mashed cannellini beans give these balls a hearty and comforting bite, and a hidden burst of melty mozzarella winks hello just when you didn't think you needed anything more.

1. Place the grated zucchini in a large mesh strainer and toss with the salt. Set the strainer in the sink and let the zucchini drain for 30 minutes. Pile the drained zucchini onto a clean kitchen towel, gather the corners, and squeeze hard to release all the excess liquid. (You'll be shocked how much water comes out.)

2. Place the cannellini beans in a large bowl and use a potato masher or wooden spoon to roughly mash them. Add the drained zucchini, eggs, breadcrumbs, raisins, pine nuts (if using), Parmesan, basil, mint, black pepper, and pepper flakes. Use your hands to combine well into a cohesive mixture that's slightly sticky.

3. Scoop 2 rounded tablespoons (or a rounded ⅛ cup) of the mixture into the palm of your hand, set a mozzarella pearl into the center, and roll the mixture around the mozzarella to create a ball covering the cheese. Place on a rimmed sheet pan. Repeat with the remaining mixture to make 24 balls total.

4. In a large skillet, heat the olive oil over medium heat. When the oil is shimmering, add half of the veggie balls. Cook, turning occasionally, until golden brown, 6 to 8 minutes total. Return to the sheet pan and repeat with the second batch.

5. Drain the skillet and return it to medium heat. Add the marinara and ½ cup water. Nestle the fried veggie balls into the marinara. When the marinara begins to gently bubble, reduce the heat to low. Simmer for about 10 minutes, flipping the veggie balls halfway, until the mozzarella centers are warmed through and gooey. (There's only one way to test this: you know what to do.) Serve family style with garlic bread, if you like.

Four-Cheese Lasagna

Serves 8 to 10

Extra-virgin olive oil

Kosher salt

1 pound lasagna noodles (not no-boil)

32 ounces whole-milk ricotta

16 ounces shredded mozzarella cheese

10 ounces goat cheese

1 cup freshly grated Parmesan or pecorino cheese, plus more for topping

1 cup chopped fresh mint

Freshly ground black pepper

Red pepper flakes

4 cups Grossy's Marinara (page 153) or store-bought marinara sauce

Garlic bread (see page 152), for serving (optional)

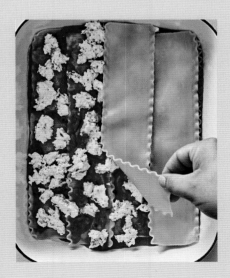

As the saying goes, "Live. Laugh. Lasagna." And, honestly, if there is anything you can be sure I'm doing at any given moment, it's exactly that. I have been making this lasagna for dinner parties probably since the very first one I threw. It's a great foundation recipe that can be customized with the addition of crumbled sausage or diced veggies. But the classic four-cheese version facilitates incredible conversation around the table while you force people to guess what the secret fourth cheese is. (It's tangy goat cheese, which almost no one ever gets right!) Bubbling through its core, crispy around the edges, drowning in marinara, and oozing with cheese, this dish is an instant crowd-pleaser and a guaranteed way to make delicious memories.

1. Preheat the oven to 350°F. Grease a 9 x 13-inch baking dish with olive oil.

2. Bring a large pot of salted water to a boil over high heat. Add the lasagna noodles and cook to al dente according to the package directions. Drain and toss with olive oil to prevent sticking.

3. Meanwhile, in a large bowl, combine the ricotta, mozzarella, goat cheese, Parmesan, and mint. Season with salt, black pepper, and pepper flakes. Stir to combine well.

4. Spread about ½ cup marinara over the bottom of the baking dish. Add enough lasagna noodles to create a completely covered layer, overlapping if necessary. Spread about 1 cup marinara over the noodles, then drop about a third of the cheese mixture over top. Add another layer of noodles and repeat the process two more times, ending with a final layer of noodles. Top with the remaining ½ cup marinara and blanket the top with plenty of Parmesan.

5. Bake for 30 to 40 minutes, until the cheese is golden brown and the edges of the lasagna are crispy. Remove from the oven and let cool in the baking dish for about 10 minutes before slicing and serving, ideally alongside garlic bread, if you like.

Note

No kitchen is complete without at least one lasagna in the freezer at all times! See page 15 for a guide to successful storage.

Eggplant Parmesan

Serves 6

2 large globe eggplants

Kosher salt

1 cup all-purpose flour

2 large eggs

Extra-virgin olive oil, for frying

4 cups Grossy's Marinara (page 153) or store-bought marinara

2 cups freshly grated Parmesan cheese

16 ounces mozzarella cheese, thinly sliced

Garlic bread (see page 152), for serving (optional)

As an Italian American, eating eggplant parmesan is as natural and frequent as breathing. This classic Italian dish might as well flow out of our sink faucets—that's how much consumption occurs. This version, like many of my recipes, is my take, based on all the recipes I grew up eating, most of which called for eggplant dredged in breadcrumbs, then fried up. I find breadcrumbs to be a bit heavy and grainy when they are smothered in all that marinara and cheese, so instead, I fry mine in a mix of egg and flour, which makes them super light and crunchy. I always fry some extra eggplant to snack on while making my parm, and that, my friend, is my hottest tip.

1. First, we need to sweat the eggplant. Trust the process, ignore the name. Line a rimmed sheet pan with paper towels and have more paper towels at the ready. Slice the eggplant into ½-inch-thick rounds and arrange a single layer of rounds on the towels. Salt both sides of the rounds, then add another layer of paper towels on top of them. Repeat with the remaining eggplant rounds until all are salted and tucked into bed, finishing with a layer of paper towels.

2. Place a second sheet pan on top of your layered eggplant slices, then place some heavy books or a skillet on top. This forces out excess water from the eggplant, preventing soggy eggplant parm. Leave your eggplant to sweat for at least 20 minutes or up to 1 hour. If you do it right, the paper towels will be totally wet when you pull off the layers. When the eggplant is done sweating, pat every piece completely dry with fresh paper towels and stack the rounds. Wipe the rimmed sheet pan dry and line it with fresh paper towels.

3. Preheat the oven to 350°F.

4. Meanwhile, set up your dredging station. Place the flour in one shallow bowl and beat the eggs in a second shallow bowl.

5. Keeping one hand dry and letting the other get wet, drag one piece of eggplant through the flour, shaking off any excess. Dredge it in the eggs, letting any excess drip off. Then place it back in the flour mixture, gently pressing to adhere an even layer of flour all over and letting any excess fall away. Place the coated eggplant on a large plate and repeat with 3 or 4 more slices until the plate is full.

6. In a large oven-safe skillet, heat a ¼-inch layer of olive oil over medium heat. When the oil is shimmering, use tongs to add the coated eggplant, taking care not to crowd the skillet. Cook until the outside is crisp and golden brown, 2 to 3 minutes per side. (Remember, the eggplant does not cook fully here.) Transfer the fried eggplant to the prepared sheet pan.

7. Repeat the dredging and crisping, wiping out the skillet and heating fresh oil between each batch.

8. Wipe the skillet completely clean, then spread 1 cup of the marinara over the bottom. Add a single layer of eggplant, followed by another cup of the sauce, ⅔ cup Parmesan, and about a third of the mozzarella. Repeat this layering two more times, using up the remaining eggplant, marinara, Parmesan, and mozzarella. Clean and dry the rimmed sheet pan, then place the skillet on top and slide into the oven.

9. Bake for 30 to 45 minutes, until the cheese is bubbly and browned. Serve warm, ideally with some hunks of garlic bread, if you like.

Prosciutto & Mozzarella–Stuffed Chicken Parm

Serves 6

2 pounds boneless, skinless chicken breasts, pounded thin

Kosher salt and freshly ground black pepper

16 ounces sliced mozzarella

3 ounces thinly sliced prosciutto

1 cup all-purpose flour

2 large eggs

2 tablespoons spicy brown mustard

1 cup panko breadcrumbs

2½ cups freshly grated Parmesan cheese

Zest of 1 lemon

1 cup extra-virgin olive oil

2 cups Grossy's Marinara (page 153) or store-bought marinara, plus more for serving

2 cups shredded mozzarella

Cooked spaghetti, for serving

Garlic bread (see page 152), for serving (optional)

Throughout my life, one of my favorite pastimes has been making all of my friends' mothers fall deeply in love with me, especially the Italian American ones. As soon as they grab my cheeks and give them a pinch, I know I'm golden. Julia, one of my best friends from college, invited me to her family's house down the Jersey shore one summer—and as soon as I met her mother, Cynthia, I felt immediately at home. Within seconds we were in the kitchen cooking; Cynthia and Julia taught me how to make their family's prosciutto and mozzarella–stuffed chicken, which they had been making together since Julia was old enough to cook. I had never had such delicious cutlets, perfectly crispy on the outside with salty bites of prosciutto keeping the chicken moist and molten mozz oozing out from the inside. They're great on their own, so feel free to stop there, but when you add marinara and use them as the foundation for chicken parm . . . the classic rises to a new level.

1. Line a rimmed sheet pan with foil and fit a wire rack on top of it.

2. Pat the chicken dry with paper towels and season generously with salt and pepper. Lay two slices of mozzarella on top of each breast, then drape a slice of prosciutto over the mozz. Press the prosciutto onto the edge of the chicken breast to adhere.

3. Set up your dredging station. Place the flour in a shallow bowl. In a second shallow bowl, beat the eggs with the mustard. In a third shallow bowl, combine the panko, ½ cup of the parmesan, the lemon zest, and a big pinch each of salt and pepper and use your hands to mix it all together. Line up the plates in this order, from left to right: flour, eggs, panko.

4. Keeping one hand dry and letting the other get wet, add one cutlet to the flour, turning to coat and shaking off any excess. Dredge it in the egg mixture, letting any excess drip off. Then place the cutlet in the panko mixture, patting to adhere crumbs all over and letting any excess fall away. Place the coated cutlet on a plate or a second empty sheet pan and repeat with the remaining cutlets.

5. In a large skillet, heat about ½ inch of oil over medium heat for 6 to 8 minutes. (Sprinkle some panko in the oil. If it starts sizzling immediately, your oil is ready to go.)

6. Use tongs to carefully lower 1 or 2 cutlets into the oil. You want them to have plenty of room to express themselves, so don't pack them in. Cook, using the tongs to flip the cutlets and move them around in the oil, until deep golden brown and very crisp, 4 to 5 minutes per side. (There will be hot spots and you want these girls to tan evenly!) Transfer the fried cutlets to the wire rack. Repeat with the remaining cutlets, adding more oil to the skillet as needed.

7. Turn the broiler to high.

8. Spoon 2 to 3 tablespoons of marinara over each cutlet on the wire rack. Top each one with about ¼ cup shredded mozzarella and ¼ cup Parmesan. Broil for 3 to 5 minutes, until the cheese is browned and bubbly. (Stay vigilant because they broil fast!)

9. Serve each cutlet with a pile of spaghetti, a plate of garlic bread (if you like), and plenty more of the warm marinara.

Sunday Ragù

Serves 6 to 8

8 cups Grossy's Marinara (page 153) or store-bought marinara

1½ pounds flank steak or sliced braciole

Kosher salt and freshly ground black pepper

½ cup Homemade Breadcrumbs (page 33) or store-bought panko breadcrumbs

½ cup raisins

¼ cup freshly grated Parmesan or pecorino cheese

¼ cup finely chopped fresh parsley

2 to 3 pounds bone-in pork shoulder

1 pound Italian sausage links

1 (2-inch) piece pepperoni

Garlic bread (see page 152), for serving (optional)

Note

Sliced braciole is traditionally used in this dish, but flank steak is a perfect, more widely available alternative. Even if you use flank, once it's stuffed, rolled, and tied, it's still called braciole!

A meat-filled ragù is like the *RuPaul's Drag Race* of a Sunday dinner. Everyone in the family makes it with the highest levels of extravaganza. Italian sausage is always in the top 4, no question. Pork is there, too, showing off her shoulder. Braciole is on the runway, ready to do a sickening reveal from what you think is just beef to a stuffing of breadcrumbs, Parmesan, and raisins. Gasp! In my family, Bimpy always rooted for pig's feet, but Grandma Katherine said sashay away. Grandma Millie, on the other hand, stole the entire show with the pepperoni chunk underdog, which she would death drop into her ragù the same way you might drop a Parmesan rind into your soup. No matter who is in your season(ing), you're a winner, baby!

1. In a large pot, heat the marinara, covered, over medium heat. You want a gentle simmer.

2. Meanwhile, cut kitchen twine into two 12-inch pieces and four 8-inch pieces. Center the 12-inch pieces across the long side of a cutting board and center the 8-inch pieces across the short side.

3. Season the steak on both sides with salt and pepper. Lay the steak on top of the twine on the cutting board and lightly pound to even out its thickness. (If using sliced braciole steak, overlap the slices to make one piece.) Sprinkle the breadcrumbs over the entire surface of the steak, then add the raisins, Parmesan, and parsley. Beginning with the long side closest to you, roll the steak into a tight log. Use the 12-inch string to tightly tie the length of the braciole. Slide the 8-inch strings to space evenly across the braciole and tie tightly. Trim the ends of the strings.

4. Season the pork shoulder all over with salt and pepper, pressing to adhere. When the marinara is simmering, add the shoulder, then nestle in the sausages, pepperoni, and braciole. Add some water if needed to ensure everything is completely submerged. Return to a simmer, then cover and reduce the heat to medium-low. Cook for about 3 hours, until the pork shoulder is falling apart.

5. Use tongs to remove the shoulder, sausage, pepperoni, and braciole to a clean cutting board. Pull the shoulder meat off the bone and arrange it on a serving platter. Slice the sausages and pepperoni and add them to the platter. Use scissors to snip the kitchen twine off the braciole, then thinly slice the meat and add it to the platter. Ladle some marinara over the meat. Serve immediately with the pot of warm marinara, and plenty of garlic bread for dipping, alongside, if you like.

Pasta

In the Italian American Food Pyramid, pasta makes up about 90 percent of the triangle. Almost every meal includes pasta as the first course, centerpiece, side dish, or as a topic of conversation, even when it's not being served. Because pasta is so important to the table, getting it right is essential. I like mine al dente, perfectly seasoned, and swimming in a glossy sauce. If these requirements seem stressful, trust me that they're really not. So how can you make it happen every time?

Make sure your POT IS BIG ENOUGH

I always use the biggest pot possible because you'll never catch me making less than a pound of pasta. But even for smaller amounts, aim big so the pasta has plenty of room to cook. A crowded pot will mean annoying clumps of stuck-together pasta. Not cute.

Get the water | EXTRA HOT

The water temp will drop when you add the pasta—that's a fact—so start strong. Not a gentle boil, not even a regular boil, but a rampant, rollicking, *rolling* boil. Heating the water with a lid on the pot can help you get there faster.

Add tons of SALT

This pot of water needs to season the pasta, plus it will help out with the sauce (more on that in a moment), so it needs to be seriously salty. No precious pinches here; we're talking a tablespoon or more until you've basically got a pot of seawater.

STIR, STIR, STIR

Stir as soon as the pasta goes in, then continue to stir every few minutes while it cooks. Not only will doing so keep the pasta from sticking together or to the pot, but it'll also make the water extra starchy, which is important for the sauce (almost there, I promise).

THE CUP RUNNETH OVER

Before pouring that salty, starchy pasta cooking water down the drain, double-check the recipe to see if you should reserve a cup or two. Adding extra liquid to your sauce helps coat the pasta evenly; the starch in it makes everything unrealistically glossy and smooth; and because you already salted your water perfectly, you're enhancing the flavor all around. If you forgot to save some water, just whisk 1 teaspoon of cornstarch and a pinch of salt into 1 cup of hot water and carry on with your recipe.

STOP at al dente

Check the package directions for the minimum cooking time and taste the pasta as soon as your timer goes off. It should be cooked to the point where it's easy to bite through, but still *very* firm. It might feel wrong, but know that the pasta will get more cook time in its sauce, so trust the process. If you're using fresh pasta as opposed to dried, it will only need a few minutes (like 2 to 4) and you'll be looking for a springy chew.

OIL be there for you

Some people believe in this, but I'm firmly against adding olive oil to the pasta water—the pasta just gets greasy and slick. But if you've drained your pasta and you're not ready to use it yet, or if it needs to cool down, tossing it with a small amount of olive oil goes a long way to stop it from clumping up.

THE ART OF SAUCING

Add your drained pasta directly to the skillet or pot or industrial-size vat of sauce over medium heat and use tongs to toss, toss, toss. Add the reserved pasta cooking water about ¼ cup at a time, tossing more and letting the sauce thicken before adding more, if you need it. The constant agitation will coat the pasta thoroughly and activate its starch for a thick and stunning plate of pasta every time.

SHAPE UP

The long and the short of it is pasta shape doesn't matter all that much, and I usually improvise with whatever I have on hand. (Which, let's be honest, is usually a grocery aisle's equivalent of pasta.) But a good rule of thumb when choosing your perfect shape: Long pastas are for simple, saucy dishes and short pastas are for chunky, textural dishes. Like all good rules, this one is meant to be broken, like the way my Vodka Sawce (page 193) clings to the ridges of rigatoni or how the Mushroom Bolognese (page 190) is just begging for strands of tagliatelle. Don't get bent out of shape about it!

Spaghetti Aglio e Olio

Serves 2

Kosher salt

½ pound long pasta, such as spaghetti, linguine, fettuccini, or bucatini

2 tablespoons extra-virgin olive oil

4 garlic cloves, thinly sliced

4 anchovy fillets

½ teaspoon freshly ground black pepper

¼ teaspoon red pepper flakes

4 tablespoons (½ stick) unsalted butter

Juice of 1 lemon

1 cup pitted Castelvetrano olives, halved

½ cup freshly grated Parmesan or pecorino cheese, plus more for serving

¼ cup Homemade Breadcrumbs (page 33) or store-bought panko breadcrumbs

¼ cup finely chopped fresh parsley or 2 tablespoons dried parsley

My family *knows* how to stock a pantry. Dad kept our basement pantry solidly stocked, and I certainly inherited the gene. It originated with Bimpy, whose basement was always like a proper NYC bodega, with shelves stocked to the brim when he was still able to race up and down the stairs. We would joke that if the world ended, we would survive the longest because of our collective pantries. You might say I put that theory to the test when March 2020's lockdown began, and, well, here we are. For all my fellow pantry queens out there, I'm happy to present the original pantry meal: aglio e olio. Bimpy and Grandma Katherine would whip up this dish the second anyone passed through their doors because they had everything for the dish on hand at all times—and I bet you do, too. (And if you're missing something, substitute it or leave it out!) Olive oil, garlic, and anchovies are the foundation, and then you can throw in anything else that makes sense, like pitted olives or seared scallops as a special treat. This recipe is the perfect starting place, but it's truly the most flexible, customizable, ready-in-a-flash comfort meal possible!

1. Bring a large pot of salted water to a boil over high heat. Add the pasta and cook until al dente according to the package directions. Reserve 1 cup of the pasta water, then drain.

2. Meanwhile, in a large skillet, heat the olive oil over medium heat. When the oil is shimmering, add the garlic, anchovies, black pepper, and pepper flakes. Cook, stirring to break up the anchovies, until the garlic begins to brown, about 5 minutes. Remove from the heat until the pasta is done cooking.

3. Return the skillet to medium heat and add the pasta, butter, lemon juice, olives, and ¼ cup of the reserved pasta water. Use tongs to toss and coat the pasta. Slowly add the Parmesan, tossing to combine. Continue to add the reserved pasta water, ¼ cup at a time, as needed to create a thick sauce. Remove the skillet from the heat.

4. Taste for seasoning, then top with the breadcrumbs and parsley. Serve immediately with more Parmesan.

BAKED PASTA PRIMAVERA, PAGE 180

Baked Pasta Primavera

Serves 4 to 6

2 tablespoons extra-virgin olive oil

1 (8-ounce) package cream cheese

¼ cup dry white wine

¼ cup vegetable broth

1 bunch Broccolini, trimmed and cut into 1-inch pieces

1 bunch thick asparagus, woody ends removed, cut into 1-inch pieces

1 medium shallot, thinly sliced

Kosher salt and freshly ground black pepper

Red pepper flakes

1 pound farfalle pasta

1 cup fresh or frozen peas

¼ cup freshly grated Parmesan or pecorino cheese

¼ cup roughly chopped fresh mint

Zest and juice of 1 lemon

This primavera pasta is a celebration of all the best spring produce, vibrantly green and inviting. The pasta boils away while the veggies and sauce work their magic in the oven. Then everything joins together and is blanketed in a cream sauce that feels like putting on a light jacket on a spring day: it does just what you need it to, no more, no less. With hints of white wine, fresh mint, and lemon, this sauce lets the bounty of veggies be the star.

1. Preheat the oven to 400°F.

2. Place the olive oil in a 9 x 13-inch baking dish and swirl the dish around to fully coat the bottom. Set the block of cream cheese in the center of the baking dish, then pour in the wine and broth. Arrange the Broccolini, asparagus, and shallot around the cream cheese. Season the veggies with salt, black pepper, and pepper flakes.

3. Cover the baking dish with foil and bake for 15 to 20 minutes, until the veggies are crisp-tender and the cream cheese is meltingly soft. Remove from the oven and discard the foil.

4. Meanwhile, bring a large pot of salted water to a boil over high heat. Add the farfalle and cook until just shy of al dente according to the package directions. About 1 minute before the farfalle is done, add the peas and let them finish cooking together. Reserve 1 cup of the pasta water, then drain the pasta and peas.

5. Use tongs to toss the veggies and cream cheese together. Add the drained pasta and peas to the baking dish, along with the Parmesan. Toss everything together, adding a splash of the reserved pasta water as needed to help the sauce come together.

6. Mix in the mint and the lemon zest and juice. Finish with a few cracks of black pepper and another pinch of pepper flakes. Serve.

Ceci e Pepe

Serves 4 to 6

CECI

1 (15.5-ounce) can chickpeas, drained and rinsed

¼ cup extra-virgin olive oil

2 teaspoons freshly grated Parmesan or pecorino cheese

1 teaspoon freshly ground black pepper

PASTA

1 teaspoon kosher salt

1 pound spaghetti

1 tablespoon freshly ground black pepper

1½ cups grated pecorino cheese

½ cup freshly grated Parmesan cheese

In Italian, *cacio e pepe* translates to "cheese and pepper," which is a pretty literal recipe title. Cheese and pepper are traditionally the only ingredients in the classic Roman dish, and I ate enough plates of it while living in Rome to say she's perfect as she is. I, however, would like to humbly submit the addition of *ceci*, or chickpeas. Like Mary-Kate and Ashley interning in Rome, they come in a pair: fried, which gives a little crunch, and mashed, which adds a starchy creaminess. Combined with a mountain of cheese and a generous amount of pepper, I can't imagine anyone would say no to this crunchy, creamy, cheesy, spicy delight.

1. MAKE THE CECI: Arrange the chickpeas on paper towels and pat dry. Dry them a second time to be sure!

2. In a large skillet, heat the olive oil over medium heat. When the oil is shimmering, add half of the chickpeas and cook, stirring occasionally, until very crispy, 15 to 20 minutes. Use a slotted spoon to transfer the chickpeas to a small bowl. Immediately add the Parmesan and pepper and toss to coat. Wipe out the skillet.

3. MEANWHILE, MAKE THE PASTA: Fill a large pot with 2 inches of water and add the salt. Bring the water to a boil over high heat. Add the spaghetti and cook to al dente according to the package directions.

4. As soon as the pasta hits the water, add the pepper to the skillet used to cook the chickpeas, and set it over medium heat. Toast the pepper, stirring often, until fragrant, about 2 minutes. Scoop out 1 cup of the pasta water and add it to the skillet, along with the remaining chickpeas. Let the pepper and chickpeas simmer in the water while the pasta finishes cooking.

5. In a medium bowl, combine the pecorino and Parmesan. Use a whisk to break up any clumps.

recipe continues

6. As soon as the spaghetti is al dente, use tongs to transfer the pasta directly from the pot to the skillet with the pepper water. Use tongs to lightly smash about half of the chickpeas against the side of the skillet.

7. Scoop out another 1 cup of the pasta water. Slowly pour it into the bowl with the cheeses, whisking constantly to create a creamy sauce. Pour the sauce into the skillet with the pasta and continue to stir and toss until the sauce is thick, creamy, and coating the pasta, about 2 minutes.

8. Divide the pasta among plates. Add a few more cracks of pepper and sprinkle the fried ceci over the top before serving.

Bimpy's Pasta e Piselli

Serves 6 to 8

Kosher salt

1 pound ditalini pasta

2 tablespoons extra-virgin olive oil

6 garlic cloves, thinly sliced

1 (28-ounce) can tomato puree

2 (15-ounce) cans sweet peas, drained and rinsed, or 4 cups frozen peas

Freshly grated Parmesan or pecorino cheese, for serving

If Bimpy were a pasta dish, he'd be pasta e piselli. This recipe is a true Bimpy Classic™, and it's practically effortless. He unapologetically uses canned peas, and he demands it be made with ditalini. I'm not saying you can't use fresh or frozen peas, or even a different pasta shape . . . I just wouldn't want you to upset Bimpy. One more thing: Bimpy doesn't use salt or pepper in this sauce, which is a bold move that I stand by. I suggest you make the recipe as-is at least once—the guy is almost never wrong—and make any adjustments you like the next time around. Because I can assure you, you'll be cooking this dish more than once.

1. Bring a large pot of salted water to a boil over high heat. Add the pasta and cook until al dente according to the package directions, then drain.

2. Meanwhile, in a separate large pot, heat the olive oil over medium heat. When the oil is shimmering, add the garlic and cook, stirring, until browned, 3 to 5 minutes. Add the tomato puree and bring to a simmer. Add the drained pasta and peas. Stir everything together and cook until the peas are warmed through, about 3 minutes.

3. Spoon into bowls, top with grated Parmesan, and serve.

Broccoli Rabe & Sausage Pasta

Serves 6 to 8

Kosher salt

1 pound short pasta, such as orecchiette, campanelle, or mezze rigatoni

2 large bunches broccoli rabe, chopped into bite-size pieces

2 tablespoons extra-virgin olive oil, plus more for serving

1 pound sweet or spicy Italian sausage, casings removed

6 garlic cloves, crushed

Freshly ground black pepper

Red pepper flakes

Freshly grated Parmesan or pecorino cheese, for serving

Note

For a vegetarian option, chickpeas, or really any beans you like, make an amazing substitution for the sausage. Follow the recipe exactly as written, using one (15.5-ounce) can of chickpeas, drained and rinsed, plus a teaspoon of fennel seeds. Delish!

This dish is my ultimate comfort food. If you are Italian, you know it by heart. If you aren't, you won't be able to resist its charms. In fact, I owe one of my best and longest friendships to this pasta. In high school, my classmate Brooke (not Italian) came over after school one day to study for a Spanish test, and she ended up staying for dinner. My dad made this very pasta (as he did approximately sixty-four nights each month). Brooke took one bite, and from that moment on, she was a regular at our dinner table, Spanish homework or not. Note that this dish is just as perfect with broccoli or Broccolini instead of broccoli rabe. I rotate all three and love all my children the same!

1. Bring a large pot of salted water to a boil over high heat. Add the pasta and cook until a bit shy of al dente according to the package directions. Add the broccoli rabe 3 minutes before the pasta is done. When the pasta is al dente and the broccoli rabe is vibrant in color, drain.

2. Meanwhile, in a separate large pot, heat the olive oil over medium heat. When the oil is shimmering, add the sausage and garlic, and cook, breaking up the sausage with a wooden spoon until it is cooked through and the garlic is beginning to brown, about 6 minutes.

3. Add the pasta and broccoli rabe to the sausage. Season with a generous pinch each of salt, black pepper, and pepper flakes, plus a drizzle of olive oil to help everything come together. Remove the pot from the heat and serve with plenty of Parmesan alongside for sprinkling.

Fork & Knife Carbonara

Serves 4

8 slices extra-thick-cut bacon

Kosher salt

1 pound paccheri or rigatoni

2 large eggs

4 egg yolks

½ cup freshly grated pecorino cheese

½ cup freshly grated Parmesan cheese, plus more for serving

1 tablespoon freshly ground black pepper, plus more for serving

She's got glossy sauce and crispy bits of pancetta. Everyone knows her—she's a classic: spaghetti carbonara. This dish is completely delicious, but I have always felt like it was a shame to not highlight the best part properly—that part, of course, being the delicious pork. Until now! This recipe is a play on proportions, using my favorite pasta, paccheri, which is basically rigatoni on steroids, with generous chunks of bacon. It's a thick, juicy, fat carbonara that you can't swirl up and eat . . . you're going to want to fork-and-knife it for maximum enjoyment. You might just call this one a modern classic.

1. Preheat the oven to 450°F. Line a rimmed sheet pan with foil.

2. Arrange the bacon slices in a single layer on the prepared sheet pan. (Use a second sheet pan if needed.) Transfer the bacon sheet (get it?) to the oven and bake for 10 to 12 minutes, until the bacon is crisp. Use tongs to transfer the cooked slices to a cutting board and cut each strip into 2-inch pieces, reserving the rendered fat on the sheet pan.

3. Meanwhile, bring a large pot of salted water to a boil over high heat. Add the pasta and cook until al dente according to the package directions. Reserve 1 cup of the pasta water, then drain.

4. Meanwhile, in a large bowl, whisk together the eggs, egg yolks, pecorino, Parmesan, and pepper. Add the reserved bacon fat and whisk to combine. Add the pasta and ¼ cup of the reserved pasta water and use a large spoon to vigorously fold and stir. Lots of movement will activate the starch in the pasta water. Continue stirring, adding more pasta water as needed, until the pasta is evenly coated in a thick but slightly runny sauce.

5. Stir in the bacon pieces and taste for seasoning, adding salt as needed. Finish with grated Parmesan and more pepper before serving directly from the bowl.

Mushroom Bolognese

Serves 4

2 medium carrots, cut into 1-inch pieces

2 celery stalks, cut into 1-inch pieces

1 large yellow onion, roughly chopped

2 garlic cloves

¼ teaspoon fennel seeds

¼ cup extra-virgin olive oil

Kosher salt and freshly ground black pepper

Red pepper flakes

1 pound sliced cremini mushrooms

1 teaspoon ground cumin

1 teaspoon smoked paprika

1 cup dry white wine

1 (6-ounce) can tomato paste

2 dried bay leaves

1 cup whole milk

1 cup vegetable broth

1 pound tagliatelle

Freshly grated Parmesan or pecorino cheese, for serving

So many great meaty Bolognese recipes are out there, and I truly cannot get enough of them! But in the times where maybe I *have* had enough, it's fun to explore my lifelong quest: What else can I make Bolognese out of? One excellent answer is mushrooms! This sauce is just as thick and hearty and warming as the OG, and it has tons of great texture, too. The key here is the mixture of fennel seeds, ground cumin, and smoked paprika, which gives your brain the meaty flavors of the classic. Mushrooms work well here because they cook down without turning to mush, so the final sauce has a perfect chew to it. As a bonus, your whole house will smell amazing!

1. In a food processor, combine the carrots, celery, onion, garlic, and fennel seeds. Process until the veggies are broken down into small pieces, about 1 minute. (Some bigger chunks are totally fine; they'll just add more texture to the sauce.)

2. In a large Dutch oven, heat the olive oil over medium-high heat. When the oil is shimmering, add the carrot mixture and season generously with salt, black pepper, and pepper flakes. Stir to coat in the oil, then cook, stirring occasionally, until softened, 8 to 10 minutes. The vegetables will release a lot of liquid, then dry out again.

3. Meanwhile, add the mushrooms to the food processor and pulse about 6 times to break them down into small pieces. (Uneven pieces are definitely okay here, too.) When the veggies are softened, add the mushrooms along with the cumin, paprika, and a pinch of salt. Stir to combine and cook until the mushrooms have released their liquid, about 5 minutes. Add the wine and simmer, stirring often, until the wine has almost completely evaporated, about 10 minutes. Add the tomato paste and bay leaves. Cook, stirring, until the tomato paste is fragrant and thickly coating the veggies, about 2 minutes more.

recipe continues

4. Add the milk, broth, and another pinch of salt and stir to combine. Bring the mixture to a simmer, then reduce the heat to medium-low and cook until the Bolognese is thick and just a little saucy, 30 to 45 minutes. Taste for seasoning.

5. Meanwhile, bring a large pot of salted water to a boil over high heat. Add the tagliatelle and cook to al dente according to the package directions. Reserve 2 cups of pasta water, then drain.

6. Add the pasta to the sauce and use tongs to toss the pasta with the sauce. Add about ½ cup of the pasta water to the Bolognese and continue tossing. Add more pasta water as needed, ½ cup at a time, and continue tossing until the sauce is glossy and all of the pasta is well coated.

7. Divide among plates and serve with plenty of Parmesan alongside.

Grossy's Vodka Sawce

Makes about 3 cups

Kosher salt

½ cup extra-virgin olive oil

2 tablespoons unsalted butter

Red pepper flakes (optional)

3 garlic cloves, grated

6 tablespoons tomato paste

1 pound rigatoni

1 pint heavy cream

6 tablespoons vodka

Freshly grated Parmesan or pecorino cheese, for serving

Notes

Any nondairy cream and butter will work great in this recipe for an easy vegan version.

If you're planning to reheat leftovers later, make sure you nab an extra cup of pasta water now! Save the water in the fridge and when it's time, add a couple splashes to the pot as you warm the pasta. The starchy water will help the sawce come back to life as a smooth, glossy girl.

This vodka sawce (yes, *sawce*, said aloud in the most Jersey way possible) recipe had the most humble beginnings. It's something I've made many, many times at home and consider it to be, well, perfect. During 2020's earliest pandemic days, I shared the recipe on my Instagram account and it just . . . took off. Thousands of people have made this recipe, posted photos to main, tagged me in their stories, told their friends to make it—and after one bite you'll see exactly why. Not only is it inappropriately thick (same) and illegally glossy (also same), but it also tastes exactly how comfort feels.

1. Bring a large pot of salted water to a boil over high heat.

2. Meanwhile, in a large skillet over medium heat, combine the olive oil, butter, and a pinch of pepper flakes (if using). Cook, whisking to blend the fats together while the butter is melting. Add the garlic and tomato paste. Whisk until the tomato paste is deep red, about 3 minutes.

3. Add the rigatoni to the boiling water and cook until al dente according to the package directions. Reserve 1 cup of the pasta cooking water, then drain.

4. As soon as the pasta hits the water, add the heavy cream to the skillet and continue whisking until the cream is fully incorporated and the sauce color goes from neon orange to pumpkin spice, about 5 minutes. Add the vodka to the sauce and notice the smell of a tomato martini fill your kitchen. Cook, continuing to whisk, until the alcohol cooks out, the martini smell is gone, and the sauce is perfectly smooth, about 5 minutes more.

5. Add ½ cup of the reserved pasta water to the sauce. Continue to simmer and whisk until the sauce is thick enough to coat the back of a spoon without sliding off, about 20 minutes. (It is absolutely worth the wait.)

6. Add the pasta to the sauce and stir until coated and glossy. Divide among plates, top with Parmesan, and serve.

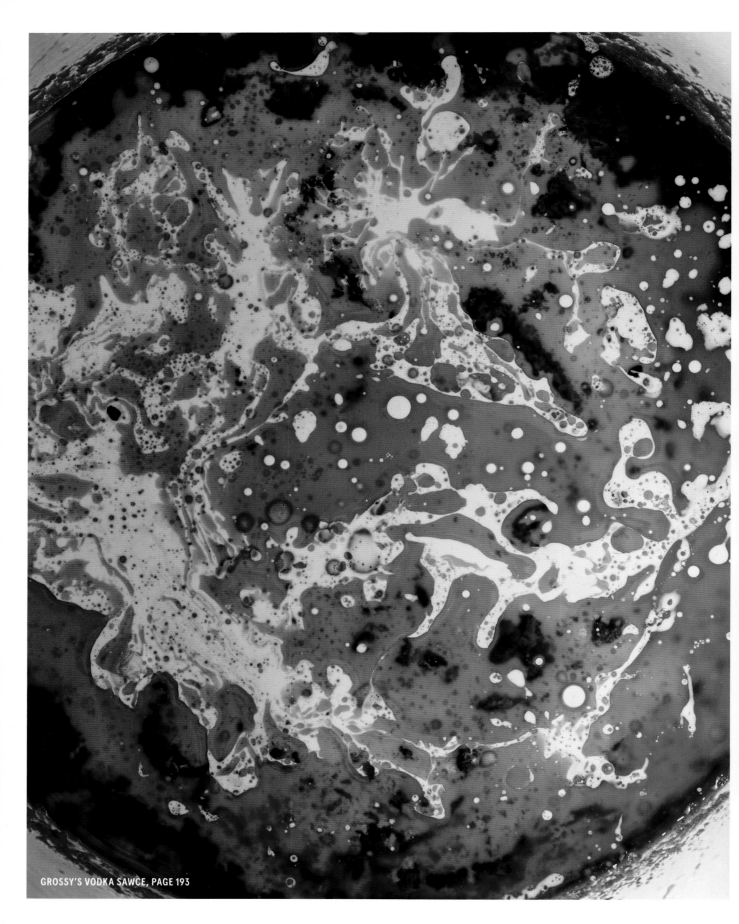

GROSSY'S VODKA SAWCE, PAGE 193

Mozzarella Mac & Cheese

Serves 6 to 8

4 tablespoons (½ stick) unsalted butter, plus more for greasing

¼ cup all-purpose flour

4 cups whole milk

2 tablespoons freshly grated Parmesan or pecorino cheese

1 teaspoon kosher salt, plus more for pasta water

½ teaspoon freshly ground black pepper

½ teaspoon ground nutmeg

¼ teaspoon red pepper flakes

16 ounces shredded sharp cheddar cheese

1 pound elbow macaroni

1 (8-ounce) container mozzarella pearls, drained

Homemade Breadcrumbs (page 33) or store-bought breadcrumbs, for serving

The list of foods that are vastly improved by adding melted mozzarella on top is long, and mac and cheese is at the top of that list. I know what you are thinking, *Why are we adding cheese on top of cheese?* Well, perhaps we haven't met. I am Dan Pelosi, and I put cheese on my cheese. Welcome to my home. Here we have a classic creamy baked mac with all the usual suspects— elbow pasta, sharp cheddar, and a pinch of nutmeg, all sprinkled with hunks of mozzarella just before it goes into the oven. The mozzarella not only adds swirly pools of goodness and a creamy flavor to complement the cheddar, but it also gives you some of the meltiest, stringiest cheese pulls of your life.

1. Preheat the oven to 400°F. Grease a 9 x 13-inch baking dish with butter.

2. In a large saucepan, melt the butter over medium heat. Add the flour and whisk to combine. Cook, whisking constantly, until the flour is lightly golden brown, about 2 minutes. Add the milk, Parmesan, salt, black pepper, nutmeg, and pepper flakes. Cook, whisking occasionally, as the mixture simmers and thickens, about 4 minutes. Add the cheddar and whisk until melted and combined. Cover the pan and remove it from the heat.

3. Meanwhile, bring a large pot of salted water to a boil over high heat. Add the macaroni and cook until al dente according to the package directions. Drain the pasta and return it to the pot. Pour in the cheese sauce. Stir to coat, then transfer to the prepared baking dish.

4. Dot the mozzarella pearls over the surface. Bake for about 30 minutes, until the mac and cheese is bubbly and nicely browned all over. Remove from the oven and serve directly from the baking dish with a bowl of toasted breadcrumbs alongside for topping.

Pelosi Family Pasta Salad

Serves 6 to 8

Kosher salt

12 ounces tricolor rotini

Garlicky Oregano Dressing (page 37) or ¾ cup store-bought Italian dressing

1 pint cherry tomatoes

1 (7-ounce) can pitted black or Castelvetrano olives, drained and sliced

16 ounces provolone cheese, cubed

4 ounces Genoa salami, roughly chopped

1 (15.5-ounce) can chickpeas, drained and rinsed

½ cup chopped pepperoncini

½ cup fresh basil leaves, torn

Freshly ground black pepper

Red pepper flakes

This pasta salad is one of the oldest members of my family. It's Italian American through and through, meaning it has never missed a single invite to any gathering, and immediately upon its arrival, it lets everyone know its heritage. The tricolor rotini represents the Italian flag, obviously. Add in some salty olives, hunks of cheese, a little meat, and a few pepperoncini, and you're basically converting the dream antipasti spread into the form of a salad. An herby vinaigrette pulls it all together for the perfect summer side or main course. If and when you make this dish, you'll automatically become a member of the Pelosi family.

1. Bring a large pot of salted water to a boil over high heat. Add the pasta and cook until al dente according to the package directions. Drain the pasta, then transfer it to a large bowl. Add 2 tablespoons of the dressing and toss to coat. Set aside to cool for about 30 minutes.

2. Meanwhile, halve the tomatoes lengthwise and place them cut side down on a paper towel to soak up excess moisture.

3. Add the tomatoes, olives, provolone, salami, chickpeas, pepperoncini, and basil to the cooled pasta. Generously season with salt, black pepper, and pepper flakes. Whisk the dressing to recombine and pour it over the pasta salad. Toss to coat and taste for seasoning.

4. Serve right away or, even better, wrap the bowl tightly with cling wrap and refrigerate for a day or up to 1 week before serving.

Pesto Corn Tomato Pasta Salad

Serves 10 to 12

Kosher salt

1 pound orecchiette

½ pound green beans, trimmed and cut into ½-inch pieces

Basil Almond Pesto (page 30) or 1¼ cups store-bought pesto

1 pint cherry tomatoes, halved

2 (8-ounce) containers mozzarella pearls, drained

4 ears of corn, kernels sliced from the cobs

1 cup roasted almonds, roughly chopped

2 cups fresh basil leaves

I am not saying I deserve an award for Best Vacation Mom, but this might be the first pasta salad in history that is actually more salad than it is pasta. It's a serious celebration of summer produce that is begging to be served poolside, with the fresh crispness of cherry tomatoes, corn kernels, and green beans all dressed up in the basil pesto of your dreams. I like to finish it off with creamy mozzarella pearls and crunchy chopped almonds to really knock this one out of the park. In the grand tradition of pasta salad, everything gets tastier the longer it sits in the fridge, so make it ahead of time and thank me later!

1. Bring a large pot of salted water to a boil over high heat. Add the orecchiette and cook until 2 minutes shy of al dente according to the package directions. Add the green beans to the pot and continue cooking until the pasta is al dente and the green beans are crisp-tender, 4 minutes more. Reserve 1 cup of the pasta water, then drain the pasta and green beans. Spread everything out on a rimmed sheet pan to cool for about 10 minutes.

2. Meanwhile, place the halved tomatoes, cut side down, on a paper towel to soak up excess moisture.

3. Transfer the cooled pasta and green beans to the largest bowl in your house. Add the pesto and use a rubber spatula to fold everything together, adding a little bit of the reserved pasta water as needed to loosen the pesto. Fold in the tomatoes, mozzarella, corn, and almonds. Cover the bowl tightly with cling wrap and refrigerate for at least 4 hours or (ideally!) 24 hours.

4. Just before serving, add the basil leaves to the pasta salad and stir it once more to distribute the flavors. Taste for seasoning. Serve cold.

Seafood Stuffed Shells with Old Bay Breadcrumbs

Serves 4 to 6

SHELLS

Kosher salt

12 ounces jumbo shells

Extra-virgin olive oil

½ pound lump crabmeat, diced

½ pound peeled and deveined shrimp, diced

½ pound scallops, diced

1 large egg

2 tablespoons spicy brown mustard

1 teaspoon kosher salt

1 teaspoon freshly ground black pepper

½ teaspoon red pepper flakes, plus more for serving

BREADCRUMBS

1 cup panko breadcrumbs

1 tablespoon extra-virgin olive oil

2 teaspoons Old Bay seasoning

Italian Christmas Eve is known as the Feast of the Seven Fishes, and the name tells you everything you need to know. For most of my life, we spent Christmas Eve, I mean, the Feast, at my aunt Chris's house, where she served at least eight kinds of fish and usually more (being extra is an inherited trait). But year after year, the highlight for me was her seafood stuffed shells. They were buttery, crispy, herby, and worth a feast all their own. She stuffed a savory mix of crab, shrimp, and scallops into jumbo shells and smothered them in an herby bechamel—and my added magic touch is to top them with Old Bay breadcrumbs. This dish gives me nostalgic holiday memories, but it also gives me nostalgic New England seafood bake vibes, both of which are always the right answer.

1. Preheat the oven to 350°F.

2. START MAKING THE SHELLS: Bring a large pot of salted water to a boil over high heat. Add the shells and cook to al dente according to the package directions. Drain and toss with olive oil to prevent sticking.

3. MEANWHILE, MAKE THE BREADCRUMBS: In a small shallow bowl, whisk together the panko, olive oil, and Old Bay.

4. MAKE THE BECHAMEL: Melt the butter in a large saucepan over medium heat. When the butter is foaming, whisk in the flour. Cook, whisking constantly, until the flour is golden brown, about 1 minute. Add ½ cup of the milk and whisk to combine (the milk might hiss and bubble; don't be alarmed), then whisk in the remaining 3½ cups milk. Bring the liquid to a boil, then reduce the heat to medium-low and simmer, whisking occasionally, until the bechamel coats the back of a spoon, about 10 minutes. Remove the pan from the heat and whisk in the salt and dried herbs. Pour the bechamel into a 9 x 13-inch baking dish.

ingredients and recipe continue

BECHAMEL

4 tablespoons (½ stick) unsalted butter

¼ cup all-purpose flour

4 cups whole milk

2 teaspoons kosher salt

2 teaspoons dried basil

2 teaspoons dried dill

2 teaspoons dried parsley, plus more for serving

Notes

This recipe uses about 21 shells, but I would recommend that you boil the entire box of shells to account for any broken ones along the way. Also for snacks—always for snacks.

If lump crabmeat is a little out of budget, just swap in imitation crabmeat. No one will ever know!

5. ASSEMBLE THE SHELLS: In a large bowl, combine the crab, shrimp, scallops, egg, mustard, salt, black pepper, and pepper flakes and stir to mix well. Set up an assembly line of the shells, the seafood filling, the breadcrumbs, and the baking dish with the herby bechamel. Fill one shell with about 2 tablespoons of seafood (or enough to pack nicely without overflowing). Dip the seafood side of the shell into the breadcrumbs to coat, then lay the shell, breadcrumb side up, into the baking dish, nestling it into the bechamel. Repeat with the remaining ingredients, making three even rows in the baking dish.

6. When the dish is full, sprinkle the remaining breadcrumbs over the top of everything. Bake for about 30 minutes, until the sauce is bubbling and the breadcrumbs are toasted. Turn the broiler to high and broil the shells for 1 to 2 minutes, until the breadcrumbs are nicely golden brown. Garnish with some more dried parsley and pepper flakes, then serve.

Manicotti Florentine with Pink Sauce

Serves 4

PINK SAUCE

2 tablespoons extra-virgin olive oil

4 garlic cloves, thinly sliced

1 large shallot, halved and thinly sliced

Kosher salt

1 (15-ounce) can tomato puree

1½ cups heavy cream

½ cup dry white wine

MANICOTTI

Kosher salt

8 ounces manicotti

Extra-virgin olive oil

1 (15-ounce) container ricotta

10 ounces frozen chopped spinach, thawed and drained, or 1 pound fresh spinach, wilted and drained

2 cups freshly shredded mozzarella cheese

¼ cup freshly grated Parmesan or pecorino cheese

1 teaspoon kosher salt

½ teaspoon freshly ground black pepper

½ teaspoon red pepper flakes

Typically, manicotti gets stuffed with ricotta and drowned in marinara, but as your resident cool mom, I'm all about shaking things up. I'm talking about a gorgeous spinach and cheese–filled tunnel of pasta smothered in a creamy pink sauce. She's a close cousin to Vodka Sawce (page 193), just as thick and glossy, but with an attitude all her own thanks to thinly sliced shallots and a splash of white wine. Making manicotti is a good group project (girl hang!) or a meditative solo task. Whichever way you approach it, the result is a bubbling baking dish of goodness.

1. Preheat the oven to 350°F.

2. **MAKE THE PINK SAUCE:** In a medium saucepan, heat the olive oil over medium heat. When the oil is shimmering, add the garlic, shallot, and a pinch of salt. Cook, stirring occasionally, until the shallot begins to soften, about 5 minutes. Whisk in the tomato puree, heavy cream, and wine. Continue whisking until the liquid comes to a simmer and the ingredients are completely combined. Cook, whisking occasionally, until the sauce is reduced by half, about 15 minutes. Spoon 1 cup of sauce along the bottom of a 9 x 13-inch baking dish. Remove the rest of the sauce from the heat.

3. **MEANWHILE, MAKE THE MANICOTTI:** Bring a large pot of salted water to a boil over high heat. Sort through the package of manicotti and pull out any shattered ones. Add the remainder to the boiling water and cook to al dente according to the package directions. Drain and toss with olive oil to prevent sticking.

recipe continues

4. In a large bowl, combine the ricotta, spinach, 1¾ cups of the mozzarella, the Parmesan, salt, black pepper, and pepper flakes. Use a wooden spoon to stir and mash the ingredients into a cohesive mixture. Scoop up about 1 tablespoon of the mixture and use your index finger to press it in the manicotti tube, filling the center, then add another tablespoon on the same side. Repeat with two more tablespoons, filling the manicotti from the other end. Set the stuffed manicotti into the prepared baking dish. Repeat with the remaining mixture and manicotti, using about 4 total tablespoons to fill each, arranging two even rows of five in the baking dish.

5. Spoon the remaining pink sauce over the filled manicotti, then sprinkle the remaining ¼ cup mozzarella on top of the sauce. Bake for 30 minutes, until the sauce is bubbling and golden brown around the edges. Serve family style.

Note
We're only using 10 manicotti, but you'd be smart to cook the whole box to account for broken ones when you get to stuffing them. Obviously, you should eat any extras while you cook.

Spicy Linguine with Clams

Serves 4 to 6

Kosher salt

1 pound linguine

2 tablespoons extra-virgin olive oil

8 garlic cloves, thinly sliced

4 anchovy fillets

2 tablespoons Calabrian chili paste

½ cup dry white wine

2 pounds littleneck clams, scrubbed

4 tablespoons (½ stick) unsalted butter, cut into pieces

Juice of 1 lemon

½ cup roughly chopped fresh parsley

½ cup Homemade Breadcrumbs (page 33) or store-bought panko breadcrumbs

Linguine with clams has always been a pasta for celebrations in my family. I make it on my birthday, on New Year's Eve, for big milestones, and often for unplanned moments of joy. It's special enough for these big moments, but also easy enough for any night of the week. The briny liquid from steaming the clams melds with a little wine, a lot of garlic, a splash of lemon, and plenty of butter to make a sauce that coats every strand of linguine. I like mine with a little kick, so I add chili paste for a mix of salty and spicy. (As written, this recipe is a medium level of spice, but you can easily increase or decrease to suit your taste.) A topping of parsley adds bright freshness, and crunchy breadcrumbs are the perfect complement. You better hurry and find something to celebrate!

1. Bring a large pot of salted water to a boil over high heat. Add the linguine and cook until al dente according to the package directions. Reserve 1 cup of the pasta water, then drain.

2. Meanwhile, in a separate large pot or Dutch oven, heat the olive oil over medium heat. When the oil is shimmering, add the garlic. Cook, stirring, until the garlic is light golden brown, 3 to 4 minutes. Stir in the anchovies to break them up a little, then add 1 tablespoon of the chili paste and the wine. Simmer until the wine is reduced by half and the anchovies have melted, about 5 minutes.

3. Add the clams and stir them into an even-ish layer on the bottom of the pot. Cover and let steam for 8 to 10 minutes. Use tongs to transfer the opened clams to a medium bowl. Cover the pot again to steam any unopened clams for 4 to 5 minutes more before transferring to the bowl. (If they're not open after the second steam, discard them.)

4. Add the linguine to the pot and use tongs to toss and coat in the clam liquid. Add the remaining 1 tablespoon of chili paste along with the butter and lemon juice, plus a splash of pasta water if needed to loosen the pasta. Continue tossing the pasta until the sauce is thick and glossy, about 1 minute.

5. Return the clams and any collected liquid to the pot and toss to combine. Top with the parsley and breadcrumbs and serve.

Meat & Fish

Cooking meat and fish sometimes feels like a high-wire act. It's not cheap, so hitting the sweet spot between majorly rare and overly dry can be stressful. Like all things, time and experience help. But I can also offer you plenty of fail-safe tricks to ensure your meat is tender and juicy every time.

EQUIP YOURSELF: Pick up a cheap oven thermometer and you're already halfway to perfect cooking. Even the best ovens can vary in heat, so preheat yours with a thermometer in the center to be certain. Also invest in a good instant-read thermometer, which will take all the guesswork out of internal temperatures. Don't worry about the contraptions with wires or Bluetooth (unless you want to)—a simple digital thermometer will do you just fine.

TAKE THE TEMP: To test the internal temperature, you want to slide the thermometer into the thickest part of the meat (it's the slowest to cook) but avoid any fatty areas or bones, so you're getting a pure read on the meat itself. If you're working with a thin cut, go in from the side toward the middle. For large roasts, it's always smart to check a few areas to be sure it's cooked evenly. And always be sure you're getting to the center, rather than popping out on the other side and accidentally testing the surface temp of your skillet or pan.

GET IT RIGHT: Cooking meat to the perfect temp is, in fact, a science. Luckily, food scientists have done all the hard work for us! Reference the charts below so you know you're getting it right.

TAKE A REST: When you nail the temp, the most important step is a nice long rest. Transfer the meat to a cutting board or plate, lightly tent some foil over top to retain some heat, and, like a nonna under the dryer after her weekly wash and set, leave her alone! The juices will redistribute, ensuring soft, moist bites. And instead of getting cold, the internal temperature will continue to rise. How long? Between 10 and 20 minutes!

BEEF & LAMB (CUTS AND ROASTS*)	COOK TEMP	REST TEMP
Rare	115°F to 120°F	125°F
Medium-Rare	120°F to 125°F	130°F
Medium	130°F to 135°F	140°F
Medium-Well	140°F to 145°F	150°F
Well	150°F to 155°F	160°F

BEEF & LAMB (GROUND)	COOK TEMP	REST TEMP
Rare	115°F to 120°F	125°F
Medium-Rare	120°F to 125°F	130°F
Medium	130°F to 135°F	140°F
Medium-Well	140°F to 145°F	150°F
Well	150°F to 155°F	160°F

Fattier cuts and roasts often need to reach higher temperatures; the cue will be tenderness instead of temp.

PORK (CUTS AND ROASTS*)	COOK TEMP	REST TEMP
Medium	140°F to 145°F	150°F
Well	150°F to 155°F	160°F

PORK (GROUND)	COOK TEMP	REST TEMP
Well	160°F	n/a

CHICKEN (WHOLE)	COOK TEMP	REST TEMP
Breast	160°F	165°F

CHICKEN (CUTS)	COOK TEMP	REST TEMP
White Meat	160°F	165°F
Dark Meat	170°F	175°F

CHICKEN (GROUND)	COOK TEMP	REST TEMP
Well	165°F	n/a

FISH	COOK TEMP	REST TEMP
White Fish	140°F	145°F
Tuna	Rare: 110°F Medium: 125°F	Rare: 115°F Medium: 130°F
Salmon	125°F	130°F
Shrimp	Cook until pink, opaque, and curled into the letter C	n/a
Mussels	Cook until open (discard any unopened mussels)	n/a
Clams	Cook until open (discard any unopened clams)	n/a
Scallops	Cook until firm and opaque	n/a
Lobster	Cook until the shell is bright red and the meat is opaque	n/a

*Fattier cuts and roasts often need to reach higher temperatures; the cue will be tenderness instead of temp.

Bean, Kale & Linguiça Skillet

Serves 4

3 tablespoons extra-virgin olive oil

1 pound linguiça or hard chorizo, cut into 1-inch pieces

4 garlic cloves, thinly sliced

1 medium shallot, thinly sliced

2 tablespoons tomato paste

1 tablespoon smoked paprika

½ teaspoon kosher salt

½ teaspoon red pepper flakes

½ cup chicken broth

2 (15.5-ounce) cans cannellini beans, drained and rinsed

1 bunch lacinato kale, woody stems discarded, leaves roughly torn

This dish, inspired by a popular soup of my Portuguese ancestors, is the ultimate ready-in-a-flash, one-pan-wonder, warm-and-cozy, ideal weeknight meal. My mom's side of the family is half Portuguese, half Italian, which has always added an extra dash of flavor to our table, and this skillet is packed with lots of it. I love using linguiça, a traditional Portuguese sausage, but any type of sausage will be just as delicious. Complete with beans, greens, and all my other favorite things, all you need is a hunk of crusty bread on the side. The recipe moves at a breakneck speed, so be sure you have everything prepped and ready to go!

1. In a large cast-iron skillet, heat the olive oil over medium-high heat. When the oil is shimmering, add the sausage. Cook, using tongs to flip it halfway through, until nicely browned, for about 6 minutes total.

2. Add the garlic and shallot. Cook, stirring occasionally, until the garlic is beginning to brown, 3 to 5 minutes. Stir in the tomato paste and cook until it darkens to a deep red, about 2 minutes. Stir in the paprika, salt, and pepper flakes. Cook until very fragrant, about 30 seconds.

3. Add the chicken broth, cannellini beans, and kale. Use tongs to toss the kale until wilted, then stir everything together. Simmer until the beans are warmed through, about 2 minutes. Serve.

Creamy Cioppino Chowder

Serves 8

2 sheets puff pastry, thawed

2 tablespoons extra-virgin olive oil

1 large bulb fennel, halved and thinly sliced

2 medium shallots, thinly sliced

8 garlic cloves, thinly sliced

4 bay leaves

1 teaspoon dried oregano

½ teaspoon red pepper flakes

Kosher salt

1 cup dry white wine

1 (8-ounce) bottle clam juice

1 (28-ounce) can crushed tomatoes

1 cup fish, seafood, or vegetable broth

½ cup heavy cream

1 pound cod fillets, cut into 1-inch pieces

1 pound mussels, scrubbed and debearded

1 pound peeled and deveined large shrimp

1 pound sea scallops

Chopped fresh parsley, for serving

Growing up in Connecticut, my childhood was spent slurping up creamy New England–style clam chowder—overflowing with oyster crackers, of course. When I moved to San Francisco in my twenties, that storied history and loyalty went out the window. I became a worshiper at the bowl of cioppino. (But not fully devout—I still loved and love clam chowder, too.) Cioppino's rich, flavorful tomato broth is the perfect accent for a medley of cod, shrimp, mussels, and scallops. I veer from tradition with a little splash of cream (you can take the girl out of Connecticut, but . . .) and a crispy piece of puff pastry, which is basically like the biggest, best soup cracker ever.

1. Preheat the oven to 400°F with two racks set in the center. Line two rimmed sheet pans with parchment paper.

2. Lay out one sheet of puff pastry on each of the prepared sheet pans. Cut each sheet into quarters and separate the pieces. Bake for about 15 minutes, until the pastry is puffed and golden brown. Remove the sheet pans from the oven.

3. Meanwhile, in a large pot, heat the olive oil over medium heat. When the oil is shimmering, add the fennel, shallots, garlic, bay leaves, oregano, pepper flakes, and a big pinch of salt. Cook, stirring occasionally, until the fennel is very soft, about 12 minutes. Add the wine and clam juice. Simmer until reduced by half, about 6 minutes. Add the crushed tomatoes, fish broth, cream, and another big pinch of salt. Stir to combine well, then bring the liquid to a simmer. Cover and let simmer until the flavors are melded, about 10 minutes.

4. Uncover the pot and stir in the cod, mussels, shrimp, and scallops. Cover again and simmer until the shrimp are pink and opaque and the mussels are open (discard any unopened mussels), 5 to 7 minutes.

5. Divide the soup among bowls and garnish with tons of parsley. Top each bowl with a square of puff pastry and serve.

Early Dismissal Pot Roast

Serves 8

1 (3-pound) boneless chuck roast or bottom round

Kosher salt and freshly ground black pepper

2 tablespoons extra-virgin olive oil

4 ounces cubed pancetta

4 medium carrots

2 celery stalks

1 large white onion

8 garlic cloves

1 tablespoon tomato paste

½ cup red wine

1 (28-ounce) can crushed tomatoes

1 large bulb fennel, halved and thinly sliced

1 pound peeled pearl onions

8 ounces sliced cremini mushrooms

2 parsley sprigs

2 rosemary sprigs

2 sage sprigs

Herby Horseradish Cream (recipe follows), for serving

When I was a teenager, my mother would sometimes send me to school with a note saying that I needed to be dismissed early. The whole thing was a ruse—she needed me to go home, turn on the oven, and slide her pot roast in so that it would be ready in time for dinner. In her eyes, pot roast was more important than my education, and I can't say I disagree. After all, a good pot roast cooks for hours and cannot be rushed. (Mrs. Muldowney, if you're reading this, please accept my apologies.) These days, I save my own pot roasting for the weekends, when I have all the time in the world and want plenty of leftovers for the week. The roast cooks in a flavorful mix of pancetta, tomatoes, red wine, fennel, and lots of herbs, until it's about ready to fall apart at the seams. Pearl onions and mushrooms soften, and herby horseradish cream adds the final touch of zing and richness. Mom would be proud!

1. Preheat the oven to 350°F.

2. Season the chuck roast all over with salt and pepper. Heat the olive oil in a large Dutch oven over medium-high heat. When the oil is shimmering, add the meat and cook until nicely browned all over, about 6 minutes on each large side and 2 minutes on each small side. Transfer the roast to a plate.

3. Reduce the heat to medium and add the pancetta. Cook, stirring occasionally, until the pancetta is crispy, about 4 minutes.

4. Meanwhile, roughly chop 2 of the carrots, the celery, and onion. Add the veggies, along with the garlic, to a food processor and pulse about 8 times to finely chop the ingredients. Add the veggies to the pot and season with salt and pepper. Cook, stirring occasionally, until a thick, paste-like mixture forms, 10 to 12 minutes. (The veggies will release a lot of liquid at first and then dry out.) Stir in the tomato paste and cook until it darkens to a deep red, about 2 minutes. Stir in the wine and crushed tomatoes and season with salt and pepper. Add the fennel, pearl onions, and mushrooms. Cut the remaining 2 carrots into 1-inch pieces and add them to the pot. Stir to coat everything in the tomato sauce and bring to a simmer.

recipe continues

5. When the sauce begins to simmer, use tongs to nestle the seared roast into the center of the pot. (You might have to move some veggies out of the way to make room, but everything should fit snugly.) Gather the parsley, rosemary, and sage sprigs into a bundle, wrap it a few times with a piece of kitchen twine, and tie it tightly. Drop the bundle into the tomato sauce and cover the pot.

6. Roast for 3 to 4 hours, until the meat is fall-apart tender. Remove from the oven and use tongs to roughly break up the meat into large pieces. Serve from the pot with the horseradish cream alongside.

Herby Horseradish Cream

Makes about 2 cups

1 (16-ounce) container sour cream

¼ cup chopped fresh parsley

¼ cup chopped fresh basil

¼ cup prepared horseradish

Kosher salt

In a medium bowl, combine the sour cream, parsley, basil, horseradish, and a large pinch of kosher salt. Whisk to mix well. Cover tightly with cling wrap and refrigerate until ready to serve, or store in an airtight container in the refrigerator for up to 3 days.

Porchetta

Serves 8

1 (6-pound) skin-on, boneless pork shoulder

Juice of 1 lemon

2 tablespoons extra-virgin olive oil

8 garlic cloves

Leaves from 8 rosemary sprigs

Leaves from 8 sage sprigs

Leaves from 8 thyme sprigs

1 tablespoon fennel seeds

5 teaspoons kosher salt

1 teaspoon whole black peppercorns

1 teaspoon red pepper flakes

Porchetta is by far one of my kinkiest recipes. Let me set the scene for you: a pork shoulder that is overstuffed with a dreamy mix of herbs and spices, then bound up and left alone in a cold, dark room (your refrigerator) for hours, only to be taken out and roasted until it absolutely cannot take it anymore and is bursting with juices from its crispy skin. After all that, we let it rest for a short while before tearing apart its soft, tender meat with our forks and savoring every bite, until there is nothing left. Now if you will excuse me, I need to be alone for a moment . . .

1. Cut kitchen twine into four 12-inch pieces. Evenly space the twine across a cutting board, then lay the pork shoulder on top of the board, skin side up. Score the skin diagonally, cutting into the fat but not piercing the meat. Score diagonally in the opposite direction to make a diamond pattern.

2. In a food processor, combine the lemon juice, olive oil, garlic, rosemary, sage, thyme, fennel seeds, salt, black peppercorns, and pepper flakes. Process until all the seasonings are broken down into a thick paste, about 1 minute. Rub half of the seasoning paste over the skin of the pork, pushing it into the scored crevices. Flip the pork over and rub the remaining seasoning paste all over the meat. Roll the pork tightly into a log and secure it with the twine. Scoop any seasoning paste off of the cutting board to rub back onto the skin. Set the rolled porchetta on a quarter sheet pan and refrigerate, uncovered, for at least 6 hours or up to 24 hours.

3. Two hours before cooking, remove the sheet pan from the refrigerator and let the pork come to room temperature. About 30 minutes before baking, preheat the oven to 450°F.

4. Roast the porchetta, uncovered, for about 1 hour, until the fat is puffy and the skin is golden brown and crispy. Reduce the heat to 350°F and continue roasting for another 3 hours, until an instant read thermometer inserted into the thickest part reads 180°F. (If it hasn't reached temp yet, continue checking every 30 minutes.)

5. Transfer the porchetta to a cutting board and let it rest for 30 minutes before slicing and serving. Store any leftovers in an airtight container in the refrigerator for up to 5 days.

PORCHETTA, PAGE 221

Piri Piri Roast Chicken

Serves 2 to 4

2 pounds russet potatoes, peeled and quartered

Kosher salt and freshly ground black pepper

1 bunch broccoli rabe

⅓ cup extra-virgin olive oil

⅓ cup chicken broth

⅓ cup dry white wine

1 (4-pound) whole chicken

2 tablespoons piri piri seasoning

1 lemon

4 rosemary sprigs

Note

If you don't have or can't find piri piri seasoning, use a mix of 1 tablespoon smoked paprika and 1 teaspoon each dried oregano, garlic powder, and onion powder. For a bit of heat, add ¼ teaspoon cayenne pepper.

Everyone needs a great roast chicken recipe in their arsenal—one that's filling, flexible, and foolproof. This is mine! I've been making this recipe for years with Julie, who's one of my oldest friends. Busy career gals that we are, Julie and I are not interested in just roasting a chicken—no, we want to make a complete dinner in a single Dutch oven. This chicken tips its hat to the popular Portuguese piri piri chicken, usually grilled and smothered in a spicy sauce. This version is covered in the spice blend known as piri piri, which has roots in Portugal, Mozambique, and many southeastern African countries, and is roasted on top of a pile of broccoli rabe and potatoes until it's juicy. The potatoes get extra creamy and soak in all the flavors, almost like Greek lemon potatoes. The green veg gets melty and soft—this is the only time I encourage overcooking it. Broccolini or kale work great as well, especially if you make this dish as often as I do and want to change things up!

1. Preheat the oven to 425°F.

2. Arrange the potatoes in a Dutch oven, covering the bottom completely. Season with salt and pepper. Arrange the broccoli rabe on top of the potatoes. Pour in the olive oil, chicken broth, and wine.

3. Pat the chicken completely dry with paper towels and season heavily, inside and out, with salt and pepper and the piri piri seasoning. Cut the lemon in half and stuff one of the halves into the chicken cavity, along with 2 rosemary sprigs. Lay the chicken, breast side up, on top of the vegetables. Cut the remaining lemon half in half again and nestle the two pieces into the sides of the Dutch oven, along with the remaining 2 rosemary sprigs. Place a piece of parchment paper directly over the chicken and tuck it into the sides.

4. Cover the Dutch oven and roast for about 1 hour, until the potatoes are extremely tender and an instant-read thermometer inserted into the thickest part of the chicken breast reads 150°F. Remove the lid and parchment from the Dutch oven and continue roasting for about 15 minutes, until the chicken skin is golden brown and the thermometer reads 165°F.

5. Transfer the chicken to a cutting board and let rest for 15 minutes before carving. Divide the potatoes, broccoli rabe, and chicken among plates, then spoon some of the sauce from the pot over everything. Serve.

Sausage & Peppers & Potatoes & Onions

Serves 4 to 6

2 red bell peppers, cut into 1-inch-wide strips

2 small white or red onions, quartered

5 red or yellow potatoes, peeled and sliced into ½-inch-thick rounds

3 tablespoons extra-virgin olive oil

2 tablespoons red wine vinegar

1 teaspoon fennel seeds

½ teaspoon red pepper flakes

Kosher salt and freshly ground black pepper

1 pound sweet or hot Italian sausage links, cut into 1-inch-thick slices

I wish in the deepest depths of my Pinterest Mom heart that I could say that this is a one-pan meal. I really do. Theoretically it could be. But according to Bimpy, it absolutely has to be made on two separate pans for one simple reason: the sausage cooks faster than the veggies. By working separately but simultaneously, you can get the veggies as crispy as you want (for me, that is very crispy) and still pull out the sausage when it's browned but before it gets too close to dried out. Honestly, the unexpected addition of vinegar and fennel seeds here makes for a delightful surprise that's worth expanding your weeknight rep to include a two-panner!

1. Preheat the oven to 400°F with two racks set in the center.

2. In a large bowl, combine the bell peppers, onions, potatoes, 2 tablespoons of the olive oil, the vinegar, fennel seeds, pepper flakes, and a generous pinch each of salt and black pepper. Toss to coat well. Spread everything evenly across one rimmed sheet pan. Bake for 30 minutes, until the veggies are soft and fragrant. Remove the sheet pan from the oven and use tongs to flip the veggies.

3. Scatter the sausage pieces on a separate sheet pan and toss with the remaining 1 tablespoon oil. Transfer both sheets to the oven and bake together for 30 minutes, with a toss halfway through, until the sausage and veggies are nicely browned and super crispy. (Cook the veggies longer as needed to reach your desired crispness, but stop here with the sausage.)

4. Combine the sausage and veggies onto one sheet pan and toss. Serve immediately, or throw the pan back in the oven to warm up for a few minutes if needed. I like to serve and eat this straight out of the pan, but do whatever makes you happy!

Live, Loaf, Love

Serves 6

Nonstick cooking spray

MEATLOAF

1 pound ground beef

1 pound ground sausage or sweet Italian sausage, casings removed

2 large eggs

1 cup AP Aioli (page 35) or mayonnaise

2 tablespoons tomato paste

2 tablespoons spicy brown mustard

1 cup Homemade Breadcrumbs (page 33) or store-bought panko breadcrumbs

½ cup freshly grated Parmesan or pecorino cheese

1 tablespoon kosher salt

1 tablespoon dried parsley

1 tablespoon dried oregano

1 teaspoon garlic powder

1 teaspoon onion powder

1 teaspoon freshly ground black pepper

½ teaspoon red pepper flakes

BREADCRUMB TOPPING

1 cup Homemade Breadcrumbs (page 33) or store-bought panko breadcrumbs

¼ cup AP Aioli (page 35) or mayonnaise, plus more for serving

Chopped fresh parsley, for garnish

We begin with an existential question: What is meatloaf if not simply a giant, loaf-shaped meatball? I've always been tempted to take my meatball recipe and just turn it into a loaf, as that is essentially what my grandparents did. Instead, I have found that my ideal meatloaf stands on its own with a mix of tomato paste, spicy brown mustard, and plenty of herbs and spices. I avoid the urge to cover the top with ketchup, as is the classic move, because I am more drawn to a smear of aioli and the crunch of a coat of breadcrumbs. One meatloaf move that I stand firmly by is saving a few slices to make a meatloaf sandwich the next day. Extra aioli for me, please!

1. MAKE THE MEATLOAF: Preheat the oven to 400°F. Coat a 9 x 5-inch loaf pan with nonstick spray. Fold a piece of parchment paper in half lengthwise and set it in the loaf pan so that the ends of parchment are sticking out of the pan (this will make it easy to lift the meatloaf out later). Coat the parchment with nonstick spray as well.

2. In a large bowl, combine the beef, sausage, eggs, aioli, tomato paste, mustard, breadcrumbs, Parmesan, salt, parsley, oregano, garlic powder, onion powder, black pepper, and pepper flakes. Use clean hands to mix everything together into a slightly sticky but cohesive mixture. Gather the mixture into a single mound and transfer it to the prepared loaf pan. Press the meat into a uniform loaf shape.

3. Set the loaf pan on a rimmed sheet pan. Bake for about 60 minutes, until an instant-read thermometer inserted into the center reads between 145°F and 150°F. Remove the pan from the oven. Leave the oven on.

4. MEANWHILE, MAKE THE BREADCRUMB TOPPING: In a small bowl, stir together the breadcrumbs and aioli until the breadcrumbs are coated.

5. Pack the breadcrumb mixture onto the top of the meatloaf, then return it to the oven. Bake for another 10 to 15 minutes, until the breadcrumbs are toasted. Remove from the oven and let the meatloaf rest in the pan for about 10 minutes, then garnish with parsley. Use the parchment to lift the meatloaf out of the pan. Transfer it to a cutting board and cut into thick slices and serve with more aioli.

Sheet Pan Chicken with Brussels Sprouts

Serves 4

2 pounds bone-in, skin-on chicken thighs

2 pounds chicken drumsticks

1 pound Brussels sprouts, trimmed and halved

¼ cup extra-virgin olive oil, plus more for greasing

Kosher salt

3 cups Mostarda di Frutta (page 34) or honey mustard

½ cup dry white wine

This sheet pan meal is the kind of plan-ahead, busy week, lots-to-do dinner that is as easy as it is tasty. It's a perfect mix of sweet and spicy flavors, with chicken and Brussels sprouts marinated in delicious mostarda di frutta plus a splash of wine to help the flavors seep deep into the chicken. As it's roasting, the sugars in the mostarda get the chicken skin nice and brown and just a little sticky, and the sprouts come out golden brown and sweet. If you end up licking the pan, I won't tell anyone.

1. In a large bowl, combine the chicken thighs, drumsticks, Brussels sprouts, olive oil, and a big pinch of salt. Toss to coat well. Add the mostarda di frutta and wine and toss again to completely coat everything. Cover the bowl tightly with cling wrap and refrigerate for at least 2 hours or up to 24 hours.

2. Preheat the oven to 400°F. Grease a sheet pan with olive oil.

3. Arrange the chicken pieces skin side up and the Brussels sprouts cut side up on the sheet pan in a single layer. Use a spatula to scrape any remaining mostarda out of the bowl onto the chicken and Brussels—trust me, you want every last bit.

4. Bake for 40 to 50 minutes, until the chicken and Brussels sprouts are browned and an instant-read thermometer inserted into one of the thighs reads 165°F. Divide the chicken and sprouts among plates and serve.

Shrimp Scampi over Polenta

Serves 4

1 cup polenta

4 ounces herbed goat cheese

2 tablespoons extra-virgin olive oil

4 tablespoons (½ stick) unsalted butter

1 large shallot, diced

4 garlic cloves, thinly sliced

Kosher salt and freshly ground black pepper

Red pepper flakes

1 pound peeled and deveined jumbo shrimp

½ cup dry white wine

Juice of 1 lemon

¼ cup finely chopped fresh parsley

I firmly believe in having recipes for a few solid classics in your back pocket. But I also like to dig deeper into that pocket to see what else I can find! Here we have a perfect shrimp scampi recipe, ready to be served over pasta, as you might expect. But I grew up in a polenta-forward household. I believe it is an incredible foundation for most things, so why not an Italiano riff on shrimp and grits? The lemony scampi soaks into the creamy polenta, for one rich bite after another. I love adding goat cheese to the polenta, which gives it an unexpected tang, but you can sub with herbs, Parm, spices, or whatever else you like. Just reach into your back pocket and see what you find!

1. Cook the polenta according to the package directions. Crumble in the goat cheese and stir to melt and combine. Remove the pot from the heat, cover, and set aside.

2. In a large skillet, heat the olive oil and 2 tablespoons of the butter together over medium heat. When the butter is melted, add the shallot, garlic, and a pinch each of salt, black pepper, and pepper flakes. Cook, stirring occasionally, until the garlic begins to brown, about 4 minutes. Add the shrimp and season with salt. Cook the shrimp for 2 minutes, turning halfway through, until they are pink and opaque. Transfer the shrimp to a plate.

3. Add the wine, lemon juice, and the remaining 2 tablespoons butter to the same skillet. Bring the mixture to a simmer and cook, stirring often, until the liquid is reduced by half, about 4 minutes. Add the shrimp and parsley. Cook to warm the shrimp through, about 1 minute.

4. Stir the polenta, adding a splash of water if needed to loosen it up, and transfer it to a serving bowl. Spoon the shrimp and pan sauce over the polenta. Serve.

Chicken Marsala

Serves 4

1½ pounds boneless, skinless chicken breasts, pounded thin

Kosher salt and freshly ground black pepper

1 cup all-purpose flour

3 to 4 tablespoons extra-virgin olive oil

1 medium shallot, minced

8 ounces cremini mushrooms, sliced

⅓ cup Marsala wine

¼ cup chicken broth

4 tablespoons (½ stick) unsalted butter

Chopped fresh parsley, for serving

Chicken Marsala is one of those rare dishes that feels like a restaurant experience without the restaurant kitchen effort. It's a surprisingly quick and easy process—all in one skillet!—that's kind of ideal on a night that's super busy but still needs a super dose of flavor. Chicken breasts get a quick coat and sear to lock in their natural moisture, then a silky mushroom sauce (accented with Marsala, of course) adds a dose of creamy richness. Serve it over pasta, potatoes, or rice. Chef's kiss!

1. Pat the chicken dry with paper towels and season on both sides with salt and pepper.

2. Place the flour in a shallow bowl and dredge half of the chicken in the flour, shaking off any excess.

3. In a large skillet, heat 2 tablespoons of the olive oil over medium heat. When the oil is shimmering, arrange the dredged chicken in the skillet, working in batches as needed, and fry until the flour is golden brown, about 4 minutes per side. Transfer to a platter.

4. Dredge the remaining chicken, heat 1 more tablespoon of oil in the skillet, and fry the dredged chicken. Transfer to the platter.

5. If the skillet is dry, add another tablespoon of olive oil. Add the shallot and cook, using a wooden spoon to scrape up the browned bits from the bottom, until softened, about 2 minutes. Add the mushrooms and cook, stirring, until golden brown, about 4 minutes more. Season with salt and pepper.

6. Pour in the Marsala and chicken broth. Simmer until the liquid is reduced by half, about 3 minutes. Remove the skillet from the heat and add the butter. Stir as the butter melts to create a smooth, creamy sauce.

7. Pour the sauce over the chicken, garnish with parsley, and serve.

Tagliata di Manzo

Serves 4

STEAK

1 (2-inch-thick) rib eye steak (about 2½ pounds)

Kosher salt and freshly ground black pepper

2 tablespoons vegetable oil

4 tablespoons (½ stick) unsalted butter

4 garlic cloves, smashed

2 rosemary sprigs

4 thick slices crusty bread

SALAD

4 cups packed arugula

4 ounces fresh Parmesan cheese, shaved

3 tablespoons extra-virgin olive oil

Kosher salt and freshly ground black pepper

1 lemon, quartered, for serving

Balsamic Drizzle (page 29) or balsamic glaze, for serving

While planning my first date with my now-boyfriend, Gus, I of course offered to have him over to my place so I could cook for him. He said no, saying that might be too much for a first date. While I understood his point, I was at a loss for what else people did on first dates! I couldn't convince him to come over and let me feed him for five more dates. When finally he did, this dish is what I made. This is pretty much the best steak salad you've ever had. Rib eye gets a quick sear and then a thin slice. The pieces get draped over a simple arugula salad—you already know there's tons of Parm in there. And because I have to be dramatic all the time, I like to fry a couple pieces of crusty bread in all the leftover steak skillet fat for the ultimate crouton experience. I wish you could have seen the look on his face after the first bite . . . you would drop everything and make this recipe immediately.

1. MAKE THE STEAK: Pat the steak dry with paper towels, then season heavily on both sides with salt and pepper. Let rest at room temperature for 30 minutes.

2. Set a cast-iron skillet over high heat. When the skillet is just smoking, add the oil and turn the skillet to coat the bottom of the pan. Immediately add the steak. Cook until a nicely browned crust forms on the bottom, about 5 minutes. Flip the steak and immediately add the butter, garlic, and rosemary. Set a timer for 5 minutes. Periodically tilt the skillet toward you to pool the melted butter and use a spoon to baste the top of the steak. When the timer goes off, transfer the steak to a cutting board. Let rest for 15 minutes.

3. As soon as the steak is out of the skillet, place 2 of the bread slices in the buttery skillet. Cook until golden brown and crispy, about 2 minutes per side. Repeat with the remaining bread. Cut the slices in half to create 8 pieces.

4. MAKE THE SALAD: In a large bowl, combine the arugula, Parmesan, olive oil, and a big pinch each of salt and pepper. Toss to coat, then divide among plates. Nestle two pieces of bread into each salad.

5. Thinly slice the steak against the grain. Arrange the steak on top of the salads. Place a lemon wedge on each plate and finish with the balsamic drizzle. Serve.

TAGLIATA
DI MANZO,
PAGE 237

Whole Branzino with Tricolore Slaw

Serves 4

BRANZINO

Nonstick cooking spray

1 (2-pound) whole branzino or 2 (1-pound) whole branzini, descaled and cleaned

Kosher salt

¼ cup Calabrian chili paste

1 orange, thinly sliced

1 lemon, thinly sliced

4 parsley sprigs

4 rosemary sprigs

SLAW

1 medium head radicchio

2 endive hearts

2 cups packed arugula

2 tablespoons extra-virgin olive oil

2 tablespoons spicy brown mustard

2 tablespoons red wine vinegar

Kosher salt and freshly ground black pepper

Picture it: Sicily, 2005. A young Italian American exchange student studying abroad makes his way to a sunny alfresco trattoria, sheds his backpack, and orders his new favorite dish: roasted branzino with a crisp salad. The weather is warm, the ocean breeze is salty, and his skin is bronze-ino. Are you there with me? No? Then make this recipe and you will instantly be transported to Italy in the summer, backpacking by the shore, dining in the open air . . . basically the dream life. In my best re-creation of that moment, light, flaky branzino is stuffed with citrus, herbs, and a smear of chili paste. On the side is a crunchy, slightly bitter tricolore slaw, tossed in an easy vinaigrette for a fresh, bright, vibrant pairing.

1. MAKE THE BRANZINO: Preheat the oven to 450°F. Line a sheet pan with parchment paper and coat the parchment with nonstick spray.

2. Use paper towels to pat dry the inside of the fish. Set the fish on the prepared sheet pan. Season the interior well with salt. Rub the chili paste all over the inside. Stuff the fish with the orange and lemon slices, then stuff the parsley and rosemary springs on top of the citrus. Roast for about 20 minutes (for two smaller fish) or about 30 minutes (for one larger fish), until the flesh is opaque. Remove the fish from the oven and let rest for 5 minutes.

3. MEANWHILE, MAKE THE SLAW: Halve and thinly slice the radicchio. Halve the endive lengthwise and cut into 1-inch pieces. In a large bowl, combine the radicchio, endive, and arugula. Add the olive oil, mustard, and vinegar and season with salt and pepper. Toss to coat well and set aside to marinate while the fish cooks.

4. Pile the slaw on a large platter. Remove the herb sprigs from the fish, but leave the citrus slices. Use a large spatula to carefully transfer the fish to the center of the platter. Serve.

Sweets

Baking has a bad reputation for being hard, confusing, frustrating, and/or all of the above. I'm here to tell you: it's not! Or at least, it doesn't have to be. More than anything else, easy baking is about controlling your environment—the oven—to set yourself up for success.

Adjust Your RACK

Even before you start preheating, be sure your oven racks are where you need them. Most of the time you'll want a rack in the dead center of the oven. The top and bottom of the oven tend to be hotter, which is great when you need that, but could lead to overbrowning or underbaking. Obviously, a rack is easier to move before it's super hot!

OVEN THERMOMETER

Affordable and extremely valuable, an oven thermometer is an absolute must for baking. Most ovens are somewhere between a little and a lot off, and when it comes to baking, you'll want your oven temp to be exact. Set your thermometer in the center of the oven and preheat, then adjust up or down to get to where you really want to be.

FOLD Carefully

Some recipes will instruct you to mix until "just incorporated," which simply means don't overmix it. Adding too much elbow grease can sometimes knock all the air out of a batter that has whipped egg whites or a creamed butter base. And because all-purpose flour contains gluten, mixing too long will start to develop those proteins, leading to tough or bready bakes.

TIME Yourself

Don't walk away and assume your sweet treat will be done when the timer dings. I recommend setting your timer for 5 to 10 minutes less than what the recipe recommends. That way, you can poke your head in to be sure it's going according to plan, and you can decide if the bake needs more time.

SHUT IT!

That said, don't just throw open the oven door every few minutes to have a look. The majority of rising happens in the first half of baking, so leave your sweets undisturbed for a while. The oven temperature drops considerably every time the door opens and takes a while to come back up to temperature, so even a small peek can be deflating.

Use a TESTER

Don't just trust your eyes to decide if something is done baking—what's happening up top or on the outside isn't always the case when you get down below. A wooden skewer is perfect for testing doneness. Slide it straight into the center of whatever you're making and pull it right back up. A few moist crumbs means that it's perfect. A wet streak of batter means it needs more time. In a pinch, you can use a toothpick or even a butter knife or the tines of a fork.

Set Your FOILS

If the crust, rim, or top of the dessert is browning faster than the rest of it, tear some strips of foil to cover the area. The exposed areas will continue baking while everything under the foil will stay right where it is.

COOL her down

Some recipes call for cooling completely in the pan or on the sheet pan, while others need to be transferred to a rack to cool. Read carefully and follow the directions. Even out of the oven, the baking vessels hold on to a ton of heat, so cookies that were perfect a minute ago can suddenly be burnt on the bottom.

Aunt Chris's Cheesecake

Serves 8 to 10

CHEESECAKE

Nonstick cooking spray

1 (8.8-ounce) package Biscoff cookies

1 (16-ounce) container cottage cheese, preferably small curd

2 (8-ounce) packages cream cheese, at room temperature

1 (16-ounce) container sour cream

½ cup (1 stick) unsalted butter, melted

1½ cups sugar

⅓ cup cornstarch

Juice of 1 lemon

1 tablespoon pure vanilla extract

1 teaspoon kosher salt

4 large eggs, beaten

CHERRY COMPOTE

1 pound frozen or fresh pitted sweet cherries

½ cup sugar

2 tablespoons cornstarch

Juice of 1 lemon

2 tablespoons Amaretto liqueur

No one makes a better cheesecake than my Aunt Chris. It's moist and creamy and light, which unfortunately aren't always words I find myself throwing around about cheesecake. After years of being let down by restaurants who claim to make the best, I finally asked Aunt Chris to share her recipe with me. I was fascinated to find that it contained one of my all-time favorite ingredients: cottage cheese! No wonder it speaks to me so deeply. Chris uses a traditional graham cracker crust, but I decided to lean on everyone's favorite addictive Biscoff cookies for extra crunch and flavor. And while Chris grabs canned cherry pie filling—which I fully support!—to top hers off, I love whipping up my own cherry topping with a splash of Amaretto. A cake this special deserves it!

1. MAKE THE CHEESECAKE: Preheat the oven to 325°F. Coat a 9-inch springform pan with nonstick spray. Set the pan on a rimmed sheet pan.

2. Place the cookies in a food processor and pulse about 6 times until broken down into coarse crumbs. (Alternatively, place the cookies in a zip-top bag and take out your aggression with a rolling pin.) Pour the cookie crumbs into the prepared springform pan and press them into a single layer along the bottom.

3. In a stand mixer fitted with the whisk attachment (or a large bowl if using a handheld mixer), combine the cottage cheese and cream cheese. Beat, beginning on low speed and increasing to medium, until smooth, 2 to 3 minutes. Add the sour cream, butter, sugar, cornstarch, lemon juice, vanilla, and salt. Beat on low until everything is just combined, about 1 minute. Pour in the eggs and beat on low until just combined, about 30 seconds. Use a rubber spatula to scrape along the bottom and sides of the bowl to incorporate any stragglers.

recipe continues

4. Pour the batter over the cookie crust in the springform pan. (It will look like a lot of batter, but fill her up to the top!) Allow the batter to settle and any bubbles to pop. Transfer the sheet pan (she's the security guard for spills) to the oven. Here's the most important part: Do not open the oven door. Bake for about 1 hour and 15 minutes, then check on the cake. The edges should be golden brown and puffy and you should see about a 3-inch circle of wobbly cheesecake in the center. If that wobbly center is larger than 3 inches, bake for another 15 minutes. As soon as the cheesecake is in the ideal zone, turn the oven off, but leave it in the oven and keep the door closed. Let the cake cool there for 1 hour. Remove and let cool at room temperature for another hour, then chill in the refrigerator for at least 4 hours or preferably overnight.

5. MAKE THE CHERRY COMPOTE: In a medium saucepan, combine the cherries, sugar, and ¼ cup water. Bring to a simmer over medium heat.

6. Meanwhile, in a medium bowl, whisk together the cornstarch and lemon juice, then add it to the simmering cherry mixture and stir to combine. Continue simmering until the cherries are coated in a thick and gooey liquid, about 5 minutes. Remove the pan from the heat and let the compote cool in the pan for about 30 minutes. Stir in the Amaretto and transfer the compote to a medium bowl. Cover with cling wrap and refrigerate until ready to use.

7. To serve, remove the cake from the refrigerator and run a butter knife around the perimeter before releasing from the springform. Top the whole cake or individual slices with the cherry compote. Serve very cold. Cover any leftovers with cling wrap and store refrigerated for up to 1 week.

Chocolate Anise Biscotti

Makes 10 biscotti

2 large eggs

¾ cup sugar

¼ cup extra-virgin olive oil

1 tablespoon anise extract

1 teaspoon aniseeds

½ teaspoon kosher salt

1 teaspoon baking powder

1¾ cups all-purpose flour

4 ounces dark chocolate, chopped

1 (12-ounce) bag semisweet chocolate chips

Après mealtime in my family meant sitting with my mom, my aunts, and their girlfriends, talking about everything and nothing (trust me, I was taking notes) while sipping coffee and dunking biscotti. Watching my mom eat biscotti was a master class: the way she savored it, dunked it, and bit into it . . . was regal. Biscotti, a twice-baked cookie, can have countless flavor profiles, but after checking those notes, it's clear that the combo of anise and dark chocolate always makes me happiest. And for those who can't get enough chocolate, there's some in each biscotti, as well as a thin layer on the bottom of each. Just one bite and I'm in another time and place . . . where the coffee is always on.

1. Preheat the oven to 300°F. Line a rimmed sheet pan with parchment paper.

2. In a large bowl, whisk together the eggs, sugar, olive oil, anise extract, aniseeds, and salt. Add the baking powder and ½ cup of the flour. Use a wooden spoon to stir the dry ingredients into the egg mixture. Add another ½ cup of the flour and stir to combine, then add the remaining ¾ cup flour along with the chopped chocolate and stir everything together. The dough will be very sticky.

3. Transfer the dough to the center of the prepared sheet pan. Use wet hands to form it into a 6 x 10-inch rectangle. Bake for about 30 minutes, until very lightly golden brown and slightly puffy. Remove from the oven and let cool for about 10 minutes to allow the dough to set.

4. Trim ¼-inch from the short ends of the rectangle, then continue cutting crosswise to make ten 1-inch-thick pieces. Turn the pieces so they're lying flat on a cut side and space them apart slightly. Return to the oven and bake for 15 to 20 minutes, until the biscotti are very dry. Remove from the oven and let cool completely on the sheet pan, about 1 hour.

5. Place the chocolate chips in a shallow bowl and microwave on high for about 90 seconds, stopping to stir every 30 seconds, until completely melted. Dip the bottom of each biscotti in the chocolate and return to the sheet pan to let the chocolate set.

6. Serve, or store at room temperature in an airtight container for up to 1 week (if they last that long).

CHOCOLATE ANISE BISCOTTI, PAGE 249

Banana Nutella Cake with Mascarpone Frosting

Serves 12

CAKE

Nonstick cooking spray

4 large very ripe bananas

1 cup (2 sticks) unsalted butter, softened

1 cup packed light brown sugar

½ cup granulated sugar

3 large eggs

1 teaspoon baking powder

1 teaspoon baking soda

1 teaspoon kosher salt

1 teaspoon pure vanilla extract

½ teaspoon ground cinnamon

1 cup whole milk

3 cups all-purpose flour

½ cup sour cream

Banana and Nutella. Name a more iconic duo. I would, but my mouth is absolutely full of banana and Nutella. This easy poke cake (that's a cake you, well, poke to make room for a runny filling) is packed with moist, rich banana flavor at its base. On top are swirls of sweet mascarpone frosting. And hiding inside is an avalanche of oopy, goopy, gloopy Nutella, ready to flood your plate with every slice. It's a low-effort, high-reward dessert (or an all-day snacking cake, let's be honest) that everyone will go absolutely bananas for! Just like when you make banana bread, be sure to use the extra-brown ones.

1. MAKE THE CAKE: Preheat the oven to 350°F. Coat a 9 x 13-inch baking dish with nonstick spray.

2. In a stand mixer fitted with the paddle attachment (or a large bowl if using a handheld mixer), combine the bananas and butter. Beat on low speed until mashed and combined, about 1 minute. Add the brown sugar and granulated sugar. Beginning on low speed and increasing to medium, beat until a light and fluffy mixture forms, about 3 minutes. Add the eggs one at a time, beating until fully incorporated before adding the next.

3. Add the baking powder, baking soda, salt, vanilla, cinnamon, milk, and 1 cup of the flour. Beat on low speed until just combined. Add 1 more cup of the flour and beat again. Add the remaining 1 cup flour and the sour cream and beat until just combined. Use a rubber spatula to scrape along the bottom and sides of the bowl.

4. Scrape the batter into the prepared baking dish. Bake for 45 to 50 minutes, until a tester inserted into the center of the cake comes out clean.

ingredients and recipe continue

FILLING

1 (26.5-ounce) container Nutella

½ cup whole milk

FROSTING

½ cup (1 stick) unsalted butter, softened

3 cups powdered sugar

1 (16-ounce) container mascarpone

1 teaspoon pure vanilla extract

½ teaspoon kosher salt

5. MAKE THE FILLING: As soon as the cake comes out of the oven, in a medium saucepan, combine the Nutella and milk over medium heat. Cook, whisking, until you have a fully combined, runny sauce. Remove the pan from the heat. Use the handle of a wooden spoon to poke large holes all over the cake. Pour the Nutella mixture over the cake, letting it sink into the holes. Let the cake cool completely in the baking dish, about 2 hours.

6. MAKE THE FROSTING: In the bowl of a stand mixer fitted with the whisk attachment (or a large bowl if using a handheld mixer), combine the butter and powdered sugar. Starting on low speed and increasing to medium, beat until a light and fluffy mixture forms, about 2 minutes. Add the mascarpone, vanilla, and salt and continue beating until combined, about 2 minutes more. Scoop and spread the frosting over the top of the cooled cake.

7. Transfer to the refrigerator to chill for at least 2 hours before serving. Cover any leftovers with cling wrap and store refrigerated for up to 4 days.

Italian Holiday Cookies

Makes 6 dozen

COOKIES

6 cups all-purpose flour

2 rounded tablespoons baking powder

¼ teaspoon kosher salt

2 cups granulated sugar

¾ cup (1½ sticks) unsalted butter or ¾ cup shortening, at room temperature

2 large eggs

2 teaspoons almond extract

1 teaspoon pure vanilla extract

1½ cups whole milk

You know this girl. She shows up to every party, invited or not. She's always wearing a different festive outfit and has an elusive and unique flavor profile that's sometimes hard to nail down. Truth be told, no holiday party would be complete without her there. She is the classic Italian cookie. Your family may call her anginetti cookies or drop cookies, and you might even flavor her with a combo of extracts like anise, lemon, almond, or vanilla. This Italian holiday cookie recipe answers to any name and can wear any of those outfits or combination of them. Once you invite her to your holiday party, you won't be able to have another without her!

1. MAKE THE COOKIES: Preheat the oven to 350°F. Line two sheet pans with parchment paper.

2. In a large bowl, sift together the flour, baking powder, and salt.

3. In a stand mixer fitted with the paddle attachment (or a large bowl if using a handheld mixer), combine the granulated sugar and butter. Beat on medium speed until a fluffy, pale-yellow mixture forms, 3 to 4 minutes. Add the eggs, almond extract, and vanilla. Beat on low until combined, about 2 minutes.

4. Add ½ cup of the milk and beat on low until just combined, about 30 seconds. Add a third of the dry ingredients and mix again until just combined, about 30 seconds. Continue alternating between the milk and dry ingredients until everything is combined. The batter will be very sticky.

5. Using a floured tablespoon or cookie scoop, scoop out 12 balls of dough, rolling each into a perfect-ish ball, and placing them on one of the prepared sheet pans, spacing them 2 inches apart. Bake for about 10 minutes, until the cookies are lightly golden on the bottom and slightly cracked on top. Transfer the cookies to a wire rack to cool completely. Repeat with the remaining batter. While each batch of cookies is in the oven, scoop the next batch onto the other prepared sheet pan, making sure the sheet pans have cooled down a bit before adding more dough.

ingredients and recipe continue

ICING

2 cups powdered sugar

2 teaspoons almond extract

2 teaspoons pure vanilla extract

Food coloring (optional)

Sprinkles (optional)

6. MEANWHILE, MAKE THE ICING: In a medium bowl, combine the powdered sugar, almond extract, and vanilla. Slowly add water, 1 tablespoon at a time, and whisk to combine into a slightly runny frosting. If you want to add color, separate the icing into small bowls and whisk one drop of food coloring into each bowl.

7. Place the wire rack with cookies on a sheet pan or piece of parchment paper. Dunk each cookie into the icing and set back on the wire rack. Sprinkle immediately with sprinkles (if using). Let the icing dry completely before eating, sharing, shipping, or storing. Transfer any leftovers to an airtight container and add a slice of sandwich bread to the container to keep the cookies soft. Store at room temperature for up to 2 weeks, swapping out the bread as it goes stale.

Filhoses

Makes 5 dozen

4½ cups all-purpose flour

2 teaspoons kosher salt

3 large eggs

1½ cups whole milk

½ cup pumpkin puree

6 tablespoons unsalted butter, melted and cooled

2 tablespoons extra-virgin olive oil

2 tablespoons whiskey or dark rum

1 (¼-ounce) packet active dry yeast

3 quarts vegetable oil, for frying

¼ cup ground cinnamon

1 cup sugar

Filhoses, or *filhó*, are a traditional Portuguese sweet fritter containing pumpkin and whiskey and rolled in cinnamon and sugar. They are a cousin to the slightly more popular malasada. This recipe comes from my mom's side of the family, who are from Portugal. My Portuguese aunts and great-aunts have been making this recipe for years. They are perfect for gatherings and parties—literally everyone loves them, and we never have leftovers! Sometimes my mom comes to Brooklyn to make these with me because we need to summon as much Portuguese energy as possible. We usually hop on the phone for a quick consultation with my aunt Christine and my cousin Dolores, who get together regularly to make filhó and, according to them, no one makes them better!

1. Grab the biggest bowl in your house, and combine the flour and salt in it. In a separate medium bowl, beat the eggs. Whisk in the milk, pumpkin, butter, olive oil, and whiskey.

2. In a small bowl, stir the yeast into 1 cup warm tap water. Let the yeast bloom for about 5 minutes. Add the yeast mixture and egg mixture to the dry ingredients. Using a wooden spoon, stir for about 5 minutes, first to combine the ingredients and then to knead the dough. (This dough is extremely sticky, so a wooden spoon will work better then hand-kneading.)

3. Place the bowl of dough in a warm spot to let it rise until doubled in size, about 1 hour. Then use the wooden spoon to beat the dough back down to its original size.

4. Clip a deep-fry thermometer to the side of a large Dutch oven and set it over medium-high heat. Add the vegetable oil and heat it to 375°F.

5. Meanwhile, fit a wire rack into a rimmed sheet pan and line the rack with paper towels. In a medium bowl, whisk the cinnamon and sugar together. Have both of these close to your oil so you can multitask, or invite a friend to come help! Better yet, call my mom, aunt Christine, and/or cousin Dolores—they will help you!

recipe continues

6. When the oil is ready, use a big spoon to scoop up about 3 tablespoons of dough. Use a spatula to carefully slide the dough off the spoon into the oil. Add 3 to 4 scoops at a time to the oil, taking care not to overcrowd. Cook, flipping halfway through, until the filhoses are puffy and golden brown, 4 to 5 minutes. Use tongs or a spider strainer to transfer the filhoses to the prepared rack to drain. Toss the finished filhoses in the cinnamon sugar and set back on the rack to cool for about 5 more minutes. Transfer the cooled filhoses to a serving platter. Repeat with the remaining dough, letting the oil return to temperature between batches, and swapping out the paper towels on the rack often.

7. Serve the filhoses while warm. Cover with a kitchen towel on a plate and store at room temperature for up to 2 days, or seal them in a zip-top bag and freeze for up to 1 month. To defrost, leave them on the counter for a few hours or defrost in the microwave. Toss them in fresh cinnamon sugar before serving.

Cuccidati for Grandma Millie

Makes 3 dozen cookies

FILLING

1 cup soft dried figs

1 cup raisins

1 cup toasted almonds

1 cup toasted walnuts

½ cup packed light brown sugar

Zest and juice of 1 orange

Zest and juice of 1 lemon

1 tablespoon pure vanilla extract

1 tablespoon ground cinnamon

¼ teaspoon ground cloves

¼ teaspoon ground nutmeg

DOUGH

2 cups all-purpose flour, plus more
for dusting

1 cup granulated sugar

1 teaspoon baking powder

½ teaspoon kosher salt

½ cup (1 stick) unsalted butter, cubed

1 large egg

¼ cup whole milk

ICING

1 cup powdered sugar

½ teaspoon pure vanilla extract

2 tablespoons fresh orange juice,
plus more as needed

Nonpareil sprinkles

When I lived in San Francisco in my twenties, I had the smallest kitchen imaginable, but that didn't stop me from cooking all the time. My upstairs neighbor, Vince, the sweetest (and most handsome) Italian cook, would encourage me, as he was always cooking, too. We shared food, ideas, and advice. One holiday, just before I flew home to Connecticut, Vince asked me if I had ever made cuccidati, an Italian fig-filled cookie that I somehow had never heard of. He shared his recipe and I wound up with a giant tin of them in my lap to bring to my family. My grandma Millie took one bite and started crying. Like, actually weeping. To my surprise, her mother made them every Christmas, and she hadn't thought about them or eaten them in years. She immediately thumbed through her recipe box and found her mother's handwritten version. Needless to say, cuccidati became a Christmas staple in my family, always made by yours truly. They are a little bit of a project—definitely a good time to invite the girls over to help—but the balance of spices, the soft chewy texture, and drizzle of icing over the crumby cookie make the work totally worth it.

1. MAKE THE FILLING: In a food processor, combine the figs, raisins, almonds, walnuts, brown sugar, orange zest and juice, lemon zest and juice, vanilla, cinnamon, cloves, and nutmeg. Process, stopping to scrape down the sides as needed, until everything is mixed into a chunky paste, about 1 minute. Scrape the filling into a large zip-top bag and refrigerate until ready to use, or up to 2 days.

2. MAKE THE DOUGH: In the same food processor (no need to clean it out), combine the flour, granulated sugar, baking powder, and salt. Pulse to mix well, about 4 times. Add the butter pieces and pulse again until a crumbly dough forms, about 8 times. Add the egg and milk and process for about 30 seconds until the dough clumps into a ball. Scrape out the dough and any crumbly pieces onto a clean work surface and knead 2 or 3 times to form into a single ball of dough. Press into a thick disk, then wrap tightly in cling wrap. Refrigerate until very firm, at least 8 hours or up to 2 days.

3. Preheat the oven to 350°F. Line a rimmed sheet pan with parchment paper.

recipe continues

4. Lightly flour a clean work surface and unwrap the chilled dough. Flour the top of the dough and a rolling pin. Roll the dough into a 7 x 18-inch rectangle. Cut the rectangle into six 3-inch-wide strips.

5. Trim a ½-inch corner off the bag of filling and pipe the filling along the centers of the dough strips. Fold the sides of the dough over the filling and pinch the seam together. Roll the log to be sure the dough is tightly sealed. Trim the ends off the dough so the filling is exposed, then cut the log into 1-inch-wide pieces. Arrange the cookies on the prepared sheet pan, spacing them about ½ inch apart, before rolling and cutting the remaining strips. Refrigerate the cookies on the sheet pan for 15 minutes before baking.

6. Bake for 18 to 20 minutes, until the cookies are golden brown. Let cool completely on the sheet pan, about 1 hour.

7. MEANWHILE, MAKE THE ICING: In a medium bowl, whisk together the powdered sugar, vanilla, and orange juice. Add more orange juice as needed, 1 tablespoon at a time, to make a barely loose icing that falls in thick ribbons.

8. Dip the top of one cookie in the icing, then set it back on the sheet pan. Sprinkle with nonpareils. Repeat with the remaining cookies. Serve immediately, or let the icing dry for 30 minutes, then store in an airtight container at room temperature for up to 1 week.

Chocolate & Orange Marmalade Bars

Makes 12 bars

Nonstick cooking spray

CRUMB TOPPING

1 cup all-purpose flour

½ cup packed light brown sugar

2 tablespoons cocoa powder

½ teaspoon kosher salt

½ cup (1 stick) unsalted butter, softened

BARS

½ cup (1 stick) unsalted butter, softened

1 cup packed light brown sugar

½ teaspoon baking powder

½ teaspoon kosher salt

½ teaspoon pure vanilla extract

½ cup extra-virgin olive oil

¼ cup cocoa powder

1 large egg

1½ cups all-purpose flour

1 (13-ounce) jar orange marmalade

Powdered sugar and the zest of 1 orange, for serving

I met my best friend, Tom, in my early twenties in San Francisco. We were inseparable then and still are now. Every year for his birthday, I offer to make him a special treat. Being the domestic goddess I am, I'm not going to let anyone else bake his birthday cake—are you kidding? His favorite flavor combo is chocolate and orange, so I have spent many of his birthdays coming up with new recipes to embrace his favorite couple. These bars are some of my best work yet—ask Tom! This ultimate pairing is showcased with a soft, chocolatey brownie-ish layer, a ripple of tart orange marmalade, and a sweet crumb topping. They're a perfect comfort any day, any time, just like my bestie Tom.

1. Preheat the oven to 350°F. Coat a 9 x 13-inch baking dish with nonstick spray.

2. **MAKE THE CRUMB TOPPING:** In a medium bowl, whisk together the flour, brown sugar, cocoa powder, and salt. Add the butter and use clean hands to pinch everything together into large crumbs. Set aside.

3. **MAKE THE BARS:** In a stand mixer fitted with the paddle attachment (or a large bowl if using a handheld mixer), combine the butter and brown sugar. Starting on low speed and increasing to medium, beat the butter and sugar together until a light and fluffy mixture forms, 3 to 4 minutes. Add the baking powder, salt, vanilla, olive oil, cocoa powder, and egg. Beat on low speed, stopping to scrape down the sides as needed, until everything is combined, about 2 minutes. Add the flour and beat until just combined, about 1 minute. Use a rubber spatula to scrape along the bottom and sides of the bowl.

4. Scrape the batter into the prepared baking dish and smooth the top evenly. Spoon and spread the jar of marmalade over the top, leaving a ½-inch border all around the edges. Sprinkle the crumb topping over the entire surface.

5. Bake for about 45 minutes, until a tester inserted into the center of the bars comes out clean. Let cool completely in the baking dish, about 1 hour. Dust the top with the powdered sugar and sprinkle with the orange zest. Slice into 12 equal bars and serve. Store any leftovers in an airtight container at room temperature for up to 4 days.

Olive Oil Ice Cream

Makes 12 cups

1 quart heavy cream

1 teaspoon kosher salt

1 teaspoon pure vanilla extract

1 (14-ounce) can sweetened
condensed milk

1 cup extra-virgin olive oil (see note)

OPTIONAL TOPPINGS

Berry compote

Biscotti

Chopped nuts

Crushed cookies

Flaky sea salt

Fresh fruit

Granola

Hot fudge

Olive oil drizzle

Salted caramel

Toasted fennel seeds

Whipped cream

Note

Now is the time to invest in a really
good bottle of olive oil! Fruity,
buttery oil is especially good here.

It wasn't until I went to Pizzeria Pico in Larkspur, California, that I realized what a perfect partnership olive oil and ice cream is. This restaurant makes the simplest dessert of vanilla soft serve drizzled with olive oil and sea salt. The first (of many) times I ate it, I was delighted to find my best friend, olive oil, in a place I would have never expected to see it. While you can always drizzle some very good olive oil over vanilla ice cream, I love this smooth-and-creamy no-churn olive oil ice cream. I would even be so bold as to call it the new vanilla. When I met my boyfriend, Gus, I found out he grew up just minutes away from Pico, and he, too, has enjoyed one of my favorite desserts over and over again. Even more reason to always have some in the freezer!

1. In a stand mixer fitted with the whisk attachment (or a large bowl if using a handheld mixer), combine the cream, salt, and vanilla. Beginning on low speed and increasing to medium, whisk until stiff peaks form, 3 to 4 minutes.

2. Remove the bowl from the stand mixer. Add the condensed milk and olive oil. Use a rubber spatula to fold everything together, scraping along the sides and the bottom of the bowl, making sure the mixture stays light and fluffy.

3. Pour the mixture into a 9 x 13-inch baking dish, cover tightly with cling wrap, and freeze for at least 8 hours, until the ice cream is fully set. Remove from the freezer to soften about 5 minutes before serving. Store tightly covered in the freezer for up to 1 month.

Pastéis de Nata

Makes 12 pastéis

SHELLS

1 cup all-purpose flour, plus more for dusting

½ teaspoon kosher salt

½ cup (1 stick) unsalted butter, very soft

CUSTARD

¾ cup sugar

2 cinnamon sticks

1-inch-wide strips of lemon peel (from 1 lemon)

¼ cup all-purpose flour

½ teaspoon kosher salt

1 cup whole milk

6 egg yolks

2 teaspoons pure vanilla extract

International Bakery, a Portuguese bakery in my hometown of Waterbury, Connecticut, makes the ultimate pastéis, a flaky shell filled with egg custard. Every time my mom's side of the family had a party, funeral, or any type of gathering at all, a box of pastéis was present. I was always close by them, and it's even possible the box was in my lap the whole time. Who's to say? While this isn't International's recipe, this version takes me back to those moments with a lightly sweet, perfectly creamy custard with a hint of lemon, wrapped in a crispy, crunchy, buttery crust. These are so good, I was tempted to call them "one-bite pastéis," but I will let you decide on that . . .

1. MAKE THE SHELLS: In a medium bowl, combine the flour, salt, and 6 tablespoons water. Use a wooden spoon to stir until the dough comes together, adding more water, 1 tablespoon at a time, as needed to moisten it. The dough should easily pull away from the bowl but still be soft and sticky.

2. Flour a clean work surface and turn out the dough. Flour the top of the dough and knead it 2 or 3 times to form it into a ball. Flip the bowl upside down to cover the dough and let it rest for 15 minutes.

3. Flouring the surface, dough, and rolling pin as needed, roll out the dough into a 10 x 10-inch square. Use a pastry brush or butter knife to spread a third of the butter over the surface of the dough. Fold the dough in thirds like a letter. Flip the dough over and roll it into another 10 x 10-inch square and repeat the buttering and folding process. Roll the dough one more time, this time into a 12 x 12-inch square. Use the remaining third of the butter to cover the dough, then roll it into a log as tightly as possible. Roll the log with your hands to make it as even as possible. Wrap the log tightly in cling wrap and refrigerate overnight or up to 1 day before using.

4. Preheat the oven to 550°F or as high as it will go.

5. Unwrap the dough and cut the log into 12 (1-inch) pieces. Place the pieces in the cups of a muffin tin. Keeping a bowl of water nearby to wet your fingers as needed, press each piece of dough along the bottom and up the sides of the cup to create a thin shell that rises just slightly above the top of the cup. Place the tin in the refrigerator to keep the dough cold.

recipe continues

6. MAKE THE CUSTARD: In a small saucepan, combine the sugar, cinnamon sticks, lemon peel, and ¼ cup water. Set the pan over medium heat and bring to a boil without stirring. As soon as the sugar has melted and the liquid is boiling rapidly, remove the pan from the heat.

7. In a medium saucepan, whisk together the flour, salt, and milk. Transfer to the stove and heat the flour mixture over medium heat. Continue whisking as the mixture thickens to the texture of glue, about 5 minutes. Remove the pan from the heat.

8. In a medium bowl, whisk together the egg yolks and vanilla. Slowly pour the egg mixture into the saucepan with the thickened milk, whisking constantly to incorporate. Pour the sugar syrup into the custard. Whisk again to combine. Strain the custard through a fine-mesh sieve into a large liquid measuring cup, discarding the cinnamon sticks, lemon peel, and any other solids.

9. Remove the tart shells from the refrigerator. Pour the custard into the shells, until they are about three-quarters full. Transfer the muffin tin to the oven and bake for 12 to 16 minutes, until the shells are golden brown and the custard is puffed and blistered in areas. Remove from the oven and let cool for about 15 minutes in the tin. Use a butter knife or offset spatula to remove each pastéis from the tin. Serve warm. They're also great at room temp or cold, so feel free to let them cool completely in the tin, then transfer to an airtight container and store refrigerated for up to 4 days.

Rainbow Cookie Loaf Cake

Serves 6 to 8

LOAF

Nonstick cooking spray

6 tablespoons almond paste, at room temperature

½ cup (1 stick) unsalted butter, at room temperature

1 cup sugar

4 large eggs

1 teaspoon almond extract

½ cup whole milk

1 teaspoon kosher salt

1 teaspoon baking powder

1½ cups all-purpose flour

Green and red food coloring

½ cup seedless raspberry jam

½ cup apricot jam

FROSTING

½ cup heavy cream

4 ounces semisweet or bittersweet chocolate, chopped

The rainbow cookie is, indisputably, truly, really at the top of the Italian cookie pyramid. And by pyramid, I mean tray. One of my favorite pastimes is going around to different bakeries to taste their versions—all of them are delicious, some are an absolute masterpiece (this cookie is reason enough to get yourself to Ciao, Gloria, my friend Renato's bakery in Brooklyn). I especially love eating them at bakeries because they are tedious and time consuming to make at home. Since the classic cookie is already a cross between cookie and cake, I decided to blow things up and lean into the cake of it all. This loaf cake has all the taste and texture of a rainbow cookie but is much easier and in a thrilling scale for those of us who can never have enough!

1. MAKE THE LOAF: Preheat the oven to 350°F. Coat three 9 x 5-inch loaf pans with nonstick spray (see note). Fold three pieces of parchment paper in half lengthwise and set one in each loaf pan so that the ends of parchment are sticking out of the pan (this will make it easy to lift the cakes out later). Coat the parchment with nonstick spray as well.

2. In a stand mixer fitted with the paddle (or a large bowl if using a handheld mixer), beat the almond paste on low speed until mostly smooth, about 2 minutes. Add the butter and sugar and beat on medium until a light and fluffy mixture forms, 2 to 3 minutes. Stop to scrape down the sides, then return to medium speed. Add the eggs, one at a time, beating until incorporated before adding the next. Add the almond extract and milk and beat until just incorporated. Stop to scrape down the sides again, then add the salt, baking powder, and flour. Beat on low until the flour is almost combined, about 1 minute, then use a rubber spatula to finish mixing.

3. Divide the batter evenly among three medium bowls. Stir 10 drops of green food coloring into one bowl and 10 drops of red food coloring into another. Keep one bowl plain. Scrape the batter into the prepared loaf pans, smoothing out the tops. Bake for about 20 minutes, until a tester inserted into the center comes out clean. (The edges will be golden brown, but we'll take care of those later!) Remove from the oven and let cool completely in the pans, about 1 hour.

recipe continues

4. Lay out a large piece of cling wrap on a work surface. Use the parchment to lift the loaves out of the pans. Set the green loaf on the cling wrap. Spread the raspberry jam over one side of the loaf, then set the white loaf on top. Spread the apricot jam on top of the white loaf, then set the red loaf on top. Tightly wrap the loaves in the cling wrap, then transfer the stack back to a loaf pan. Set a second loaf pan on top and use cans to weigh it down. Transfer to the refrigerator to chill overnight or up to 24 hours.

5. Remove the loaf from the refrigerator, discard the cling wrap, and set on a cutting board with the red layer on top. Trim about ¼ inch from all sides of the loaf to make a perfect rectangle. Set a wire rack on top of a sheet pan and place the loaf on the rack.

6. **MAKE THE FROSTING:** In a small saucepan, heat the cream over medium heat. As soon as bubbles begin to form around the edges, remove the pan from the heat. Add the chopped chocolate and let it sit for 10 minutes, then whisk until smooth. Use a rubber spatula to smooth the frosting on all sides of the loaf except the bottom, finishing with the top. Smooth the edges, then, if you like, use a fork to squiggle lines on the top of the loaf. Use two large spatulas to transfer the frosted loaf to a cutting board.

7. Return the loaf to the refrigerator for about 30 minutes, until the chocolate is set. Cut the loaf into slices and serve. Store leftovers in an airtight container at room temperature for up to 3 days.

Note

Don't have three loaf pans? No problem. Bake the cakes one at a time, letting them cool completely in the pan before adding more parchment, spraying, and baking the next batter. When it comes time to press, just cut out a piece of cardboard to fit on top and then weigh it down with cans per the instructions.

Pistachio Bundt Cake

Serves 10 to 12

CAKE

Nonstick cooking spray

3 cups all-purpose flour, plus more for dusting

2 cups granulated sugar

1 cup old-fashioned oats

1 cup chopped raw pistachios

½ cup packed dark brown sugar

1 tablespoon baking powder

1 tablespoon ground cinnamon

½ teaspoon kosher salt

1 cup pistachio milk or whole milk

½ cup extra-virgin olive oil

1 cup (2 sticks) unsalted butter, softened

2 large eggs, lightly beaten

1 teaspoon almond extract

ICING

1 cup powdered sugar

3 to 4 teaspoons pistachio milk or whole milk

¼ cup chopped raw pistachios

For years, my family has been trying to figure out this one pistachio Bundt cake that Grandma Katherine used to make. We all have memories of it, we always crave it, yet the recipe card is absolutely nowhere to be found. Well, I am basically Nancy Drew. Being the recipe detective that I am, I called every Maria I know to get her take on how Grandma Katherine might have made this cake. All of them said the same thing: "You take a box of vanilla cake mix and a packet of pistachio pudding . . ." While I love this energy and the network's advice got me pretty close, I wanted to develop something from scratch that was just as easy and delicious and, most importantly, sated the cravings of my entire family. I did that and then some, and this family classic was reborn with a perfect mix of familiar and new flavors.

1. MAKE THE CAKE: Preheat the oven to 350°F. Coat a Bundt pan with nonstick spray, then dust generously with flour. Tap to release any excess flour.

2. In a stand mixer fitted with the paddle attachment (or in a large bowl if using a handheld mixer), combine the flour, granulated sugar, oats, pistachios, brown sugar, baking powder, cinnamon, and salt. Mix on low speed until combined, about 1 minute. Add the milk, olive oil, butter, eggs, and almond extract. Mix on low, stopping to scrape down the sides as needed, until fully incorporated, about 2 minutes.

3. Scrape the batter into the prepared Bundt pan. Bake for 50 to 60 minutes, or until a tester inserted into the middle of the cake comes out clean. Remove from the oven and let cool in the pan for 15 minutes. Run a butter knife around the edge of the pan, then set a wire rack over the pan and invert to release the cake. Let the cake cool for at least 1 hour.

4. MEANWHILE, MAKE THE ICING: In a medium bowl, whisk together the powdered sugar and 3 teaspoons milk. Add more milk as needed, ½ teaspoon at a time, to make a barely loose icing that falls in thick ribbons.

5. Spoon the icing over the top of the cake, letting it run down the sides. Sprinkle with the chopped pistachios, lightly pressing to adhere. Slice and serve immediately or store in a cake keeper or loosely covered with cling wrap at room temperature for up to 3 days.

Grandma Katherine's Rice Pudding

Serves 8 to 10

½ gallon whole milk

1¼ cups long-grain rice

1 cup sugar

1 tablespoon unsalted butter

1 teaspoon kosher salt

3 large eggs

2 tablespoons pure vanilla extract

Ground cinnamon, for dusting

I hold this recipe very close to my heart. It is the most cherished of all our Pelosi family recipes and is *the* official dessert of our family. (Believe me, we had a lot to choose from.) Gleefully eating this creamy rice pudding directly from the fridge is peak Pelosi. Grandma Katherine taught me how to make this rice pudding when I was young, likely because she wanted someone to help her stir, but also because she knew and taught me from the start how important it was for family recipes to be shared and learned. Making it takes a solid 40 minutes in front of the stove, so I don't blame her either way! I hope this pudding becomes a special dessert in your house, too, and one you can share with your own family.

1. In a large Dutch oven, combine the milk, rice, sugar, butter, and salt. Bring to a boil, stirring occasionally, then reduce the heat to medium-low. Simmer, stirring often, until the mixture is thick and creamy, 35 to 40 minutes. Remove the pot from the heat.

2. In a medium bowl, whisk together the eggs, vanilla, and ¼ cup water until completely incorporated. Slowly pour the egg mixture into the rice pudding, stirring continuously to combine.

3. Transfer the rice pudding to a 9 x 13-inch baking dish or large, shallow serving bowl. Let cool completely, about an hour, then cover the dish with cling wrap and chill in the refrigerator for at least 2 hours, but preferably overnight. Use a fine-mesh sieve to dust a spoonful of ground cinnamon over the top and serve extra cold.

Tiramisu Affogato

Serves 8

3 cups heavy cream

1 cup sour cream

1 cup sugar

2 teaspoons pure vanilla extract

2 (12-ounce) packages Margherite cookies or 4 (7-ounce) packages ladyfingers

Cocoa powder, for dusting

8 espresso shots

Note
With no ice cream to melt, this espresso does not need to be hot and is maybe even better at room temp or cold. I like to buy shots of espresso at a coffee shop and save them to serve later.

Tiramisu and affogato are two of my favorite desserts, but this is not a traditional recipe for either. Instead, it's my fantasy mash-up of both, plus some other fun additions. Tiramisu is layers of ladyfingers soaked in coffee and stacked like a trifle with whipped cream. We love her, but I always wish she had more texture. Using unsoaked cookies here adds the crunch I have been craving, and the cream in this tiramisu is made with a touch of sour cream, which gives it a pleasing tang but also stabilizes it beautifully. That means these can be made minutes before serving or prepped ahead and chilled in the fridge for hours. On top of that, a shot of espresso poured over anything (an affogato does it over gelato) adds a huge hit of drama, which I live for. To quote my favorite poets, the Spice Girls, make tonight the night when two become one.

1. In a stand mixer fitted with the whisk (or a large bowl if using a handheld mixer), combine the cream, sour cream, sugar, and vanilla. Beginning on low speed and increasing to medium, whisk until stiff peaks form, 3 to 4 minutes.

2. Arrange eight rocks glasses, fancy goblets, wine glasses, or whatever you want to serve in. Break and crumble three cookies into the first glass. Scoop about ¼ cup of the cream on top of the cookies. Layer three more crumbled cookies, then another ¼ cup of the cream. Repeat in the other glasses, making two layers each of cookies and cream.

3. Use a fine-mesh sieve to dust a spoonful of cocoa powder over the top of each glass. Cover the trifles with cling wrap and refrigerate until ready to serve, or up to 8 hours.

4. Serve each trifle with a shot of espresso to pour over, affogato style.

Torta del Diavolo

Serves 8 to 10

CAKE

Nonstick cooking spray

2 cups all-purpose flour

2 cups sugar

1 cup cocoa powder

2 teaspoons baking soda

1 teaspoon baking powder

1 teaspoon kosher salt

1 cup hot coffee

1 cup buttermilk

½ cup extra-virgin olive oil

2 large eggs, lightly beaten

1 tablespoon pure vanilla extract

FROSTING

2 (1-pound) boxes powdered sugar
(7 cups)

1 cup (2 sticks) unsalted butter, at
room temperature

1 tablespoon pure vanilla extract

½ teaspoon kosher salt

6 to 8 tablespoons whole milk

Torta del diavolo, which is Italian for "devil's food cake," gets its name from the implication that it's overly decadent and sinful. I strongly believe food is *never* a sin or something we need to seek penance for eating. And if there's any cake that makes me the happiest and most amazing person, it's this one! This little devil is so delicious (that's the frosting), so fluffy (that's the extra baking soda), and so moist (that's the buttermilk) that I would actually call it "angel food cake" if that name wasn't already taken. But I *am* calling this one *torta del diavolo* to highlight its Italiano flair and flavor (that's the olive oil). No regrets and, more importantly, no apologies!

1. MAKE THE CAKE: Preheat the oven to 350°F. Coat two 9-inch cake pans with nonstick spray. Cut parchment paper into rounds to line the bottoms of the pans. Spray the parchment.

2. In a large bowl, whisk together the flour, sugar, cocoa powder, baking soda, baking powder, and salt. Pour in the coffee and use a wooden spoon to combine. Stir in the buttermilk and olive oil. Add the eggs and vanilla and mix well. Divide the batter between the prepared pans.

3. Bake for 40 to 45 minutes, until a tester inserted into the center of each comes out clean (a few sticky crumbs are okay). Set the pans on a wire rack and let the cool completely, about 2 hours.

4. MAKE THE FROSTING: In a large bowl, combine the powdered sugar, butter, vanilla, salt, and 2 tablespoons of the milk. Use a handheld mixer on low speed to incorporate, about 1 minute. Add 2 more tablespoons of the milk and mix on low until a thick frosting forms, about 1 minute. Continue adding milk, 1 tablespoon at a time, and mixing on low until the frosting is soft and fluffy.

5. Remove the cakes from the pans and discard the parchment. Trim the tops crosswise so they're flat. Place a small dab of frosting in the center of a cake stand or serving plate and place one of the cake layers on the stand. Spread about 2 cups frosting over the top of the cake. Place the second cake layer on top, cut side down. Use another 2 cups frosting to spread a crumb coat over the top and sides of the cake. Refrigerate for about 30 minutes until the frosting is set, then cover the cake with the remaining frosting. Store in a cool place until ready to serve. Cover any leftovers with cling wrap and store at room temperature for up to 3 days.

Zabaglione

Serves 4

6 egg yolks

½ cup sugar

½ cup Marsala wine

1 cup heavy cream, very cold

Fresh berries, for serving

I told my boyfriend, Gus, I love him for the first time over a gigantic goblet of Cheesecake Factory strawberries and whipped cream. I know, I am classy. But even classier than the combo of strawberries and whipped cream is mixed berries and zabaglione. Imagine silky-smooth custard, made with whipped eggs, sugar, and a little bit of Marsala wine for a punch of flavor. Of course, when I make this dessert, I go completely off script and fold in some whipped cream, making sure it's extra light and airy. Then I spoon the chilled mixture over fresh berries for juicy bursts in every bite. An absolutely dreamy dessert, zabaglione is the perfect way to say I love you.

1. Fill a large saucepan with 1 inch of water. Place over low heat and bring to a simmer. In a large heatproof bowl, whisk together the egg yolks, sugar, and Marsala. Rest the bowl over the pan of simmering water, making sure it doesn't touch the water, and continue whisking until the mixture is thick and dark mustard-yellow in color, about 10 minutes. At first, it will be full of tiny bubbles, then it'll condense and fall in heavy ribbons when you lift the whisk; that's the perfect texture. Remove the bowl from the heat and let cool on the counter for about 15 minutes.

2. In a medium bowl, whisk the cream vigorously until stiff peaks form, about 3 minutes. Scoop about a quarter of the whipped cream into the egg mixture and fold to incorporate. Fold in the remaining cream in two additional parts to form a light and fluffy zabaglione.

3. Arrange the berries in clear glasses. Spoon the zabaglione over the top and either serve immediately or cover with cling wrap and refrigerate for up to 2 hours to serve chilled.

♥ Acknowledgments ♥

Writing a cookbook has been a lifelong dream of mine. I never actually believed it would happen . . . or I thought if it did, it would be printed at my local Kinko's on my dime. This book may never feel real to me, but what I do know is real is each of these people (and many more) were essential to making it happen:

To Casey Elsass. You dm'ed me years ago and told me that someday I would write a cookbook and that you would help me do it. Naturally, I thought you were insane. And now here we are, and you are the single reason the book is what it is today. You are the most brilliant, calming, knowledgeable, thoughtful friend and partner-in-cream that a girl could ask for. I am so proud of our baby.

To my boyfriend, Gus. For the first time in my life, l feel completely loved, supported, and taken care of by a partner. You have the deepest well of joy I have ever witnessed, and I am honored to drink from it. You make me smile, laugh, and tingle exactly when I need it, and then some. I love you.

To my 101-year-old grandfather Bimpy the Freezer King, to whom this book is dedicated, and my late Grandma Katherine. This all started in your basement kitchen, and I'll always be cooking there in my heart.

To my late Grandma Millie and late Grandpa John, thank you for giving me the space and tools to allow my creativity to flourish with no rules and no mistakes.

To my mom. You were my favorite person to cook with from the start. Every time we get to be together in the kitchen is a blessing. So much of you is in this book.

To my dad. You taught me what cooking looks like when it's an act of love and care. Most nights, dinner was on the table because of you, your dedication to the family, and your incredible couponing skills. Someday I will publish your famous Pea Soup recipe, I promise.

To my sister, Diana, a.k.a. Donna, for being my other half. I think you got the life I was supposed to have: a perfect husband, three beautiful kids, and a big house in the suburbs. I'm not mad, though—I'm just grateful I get to be part of it.

To my sweet Uncle Phil, my best friend, my Momager in the sky. From the minute you left us on Earth, I have felt nothing but your presence in everything I do. You are making everything you ever saw possible in me happen, and I am along for the ride.

To my Aunt Chris, for sharing your creativity with me always. From food to quilts to haircuts . . . you are always creating something beautiful.

To the rest of my aunts, uncles, cousins, Carolyn, Marilyn, and every single Maria. Rest assured that every meal I've ever had in your home or in your company has contributed to this book and to everything else I do.

To everyone who is following me on Instagram, who used to follow me on Instagram, or who is about to start following me on Instagram. The loveliest people join me daily in my little corner of the internet, and I feel blessed to be able to spend so much time with you all. I wrote this book for all of you, and I hope I made you proud.

To my editor, Amanda Englander, for gently stalking me for over a year to have lunch with you, only to reveal when we finally did that you believed in me more than most. You have made me a better writer and a better thinker. Thank you for bringing me into the Union Square family that I now call home.

To my book agent, Nicole Tourtelot. You were one of the first people to believe I had what it took to write a cookbook, and you were the last person to let anything get in the way of making this cookbook exactly what I wanted it to be. Thank you for being my person throughout this whole process.

To my manager, Adam Krasner. You are my co-captain of SS Grossy and are constantly keeping the ship on course while I am off making a mess in the kitchen. Thank you for reminding me of my value when I cannot see it for myself.

To Erica Gelbard, for sending me cookbooks long ago. You made this all feel possible for the very first time. I am so grateful we have become friends and that you are my publicist on my first cookbook. I could not have imagined anyone in that role besides you.

To my dear friend and creative producer, Kristen Poissant. You somehow keep me on track and keep everything colorful and fun at the same time. I am so grateful you are on this journey with me.

To my assistant, Morgan Yezzi. Your endless enthusiasm to be part of whatever I am doing, no matter what I am doing, has kept me alive during the process of creating this book.

To my photographer, Andrew Bui. From the first time you shot my food and my face, I knew your work felt connected to mine. I feel so lucky to have your masterfully lit and composed photos in my first book. Thank you as well to photo assistants Felix Palmero and Christina Zhang.

To my prop stylist, Stephanie DeLuca, thank you for jumping right into Grossy world and finding all the right props, linens, surfaces, and more to take it to the next level. I learned so much from you, especially about what I consider the bounds of my aesthetic, and deeply appreciate your pushing me even when I had a strong opinion (or two). Thank you as well to Sam Schmieg for assisting on props.

To my food stylist, Tiffany Schleigh. One of my favorite things in the world is watching other people make my recipes more beautiful than I can possibly imagine. Thank you for elevating my food to a new level. And thank you as well to César Pérez for expertly assisting on food styling and expertly being the cutest teddy bear in the world.

To my book designer, Laura Palese, for creating my dream cookbook. It's a perfect blend of all my favorite vintage cookbooks. You soaked in all the aesthetics I like and generated a singular and personal design to the book.

To Krista Marie Young, my fellow RISD sister. Our brands are so deeply connected there is no one else I could imagine creating illustrations for this book. You understand and share my deep love of checkerboard and vintage cookbook illustrations. I am so glad we got to work together—it was truly a dream every step of the way.

To Ashley Rebecca Schultz for making sure all hair, makeup, and most importantly, nails, looked perfect in every single photo in this book.

To Ina Garten. You are the person who taught me how to cook outside of my family recipes. You taught me what American comfort food is. You taught me it's possible to have a presence in food that feels like a warm hug.

To Molly Baz, for insisting I write a cookbook from pretty much the day I met you. For introducing me to Nicole. And for picking up the phone every time I call to ask for your brilliant advice. Oh, and for loving my sweet angel, Ben.

To Andy Baraghani. Our friendship goes well beyond the world of food. You are a constant sounding board and give such great advice and feedback. You keep me going when I doubt myself and remind me to be myself when I forget who that is.

To Carla Lalli Music, Deb Perelman, Gaby Dalkin, Rick Martínez. My goddesses of the food world. Thank you each for the constant support, wisdom, and cheerleading.

To Tom Girard, Taylor Griggs, Philip Iosca, David Sabshon, Jeremy Bennett, Edy Massih, Caroline Hurley, and Samantha Katz. Thank you for patiently watching me take photos of every meal I've ever eaten since Instagram was invented. You all secretly knew I was just practicing for this moment; I just know it.

To my roommates Tyler Smeeton and Dakota Balka. Thank you for the endless kindness and understanding as I built the Grossy brand in our apartment during lockdown. Someday I will repay you—or I will pay for your therapy.

To Cynthia and Julia DiFeo, for inviting me into your kitchens and inspiring me to be a better cook, always.

To Cath Heagerty, for letting me borrow your precious linen and wooden spoon collections for this book. And, well, for Gus.

To Chris Geremia, for getting lost in the sawce with me. It changed my life.

To Jacqueline Tris, for expertly testing every recipe in this book, sharing much-needed honest feedback and deep enthusiasm along the way.

To Heather Schlesinger, for spending countless hours in the kitchen making sure the recipes in this book are kid-tested and mom approved. Your love and support are endless.

To Richard Sinnott, for generously sharing your incredible home to write in and your pool to dive into in between.

To Gab and Tyson Evans, for being the best neighbors, landlords, and friends. Your generosity in sharing your space for my adventures is deeply appreciated, as is the offer of your kids to eat my recipe tests.

To all of the brands who generously donated objects to make this book so beautiful: @HeatherTaylorHome, @LeCreuset, @Food52, @Dansk, @Nordstrom, @HeathCeramics, @CarolineZHurley, @MaterialKitchen, @FredericksandMae, @HAYdesign, @Goldune.co, @LittleKing.Online, @GreatJones.